THE RITES OF HEKATE

From Dirt to the Divine
Dr Lenni George

For Nat, my soul mate who walks beside me in magic and in life, and Leora, the radiant torchlight who illuminates the way. Together you are the earth beneath my feet and the stars that guide me.

And Diane, my sister who made this happen.

All rights reserved, no part of this publication may be reproduced or transmitted by any means whatsoever without the prior permission of the publisher.

Text © Dr Lenni George
houseofzophiel.com

Edited by Jennie Jones

Cover image © Nat Clegg
houseofzophiel.com

Additional artwork
unless otherwise stated
© houseofzophiel.com

ISBN: 978-1-916756-37-3

October 2025
VENEFICIA PUBLICATIONS UK
veneficiapublications.com

CONTENTS

WALKING WITH HEKATE 1

JOURNEYS THROUGH LIMINAL SPACE 13

HEKATE AND HER SISTERS 56

HEKATE'S BOTANICALS 97

CREATING A MOON GARDEN 127

THE RITES OF HEKATE 178

AMONGST THE GRAVES AT NIGHT 209

FROM DIRT TO THE DIVINE 223

REFERENCES AND BIBLIOGRAPHY i

'Shall we write about the things not to be spoken of? Shall we divulge the things not to be divulged? Shall we pronounce the things not to be pronounced?'

Julian, Hymn to the Mother of the Gods.

WALKING WITH HEKATE

It's around the fourteenth century, somewhere in Europe. It's a cold and grey day, raining and almost dark. A hobbled woman, old before her years, her only companion the staff in her right hand, is journeying through the countryside. Her few years on earth have been filled with misery; born profoundly deaf, for many years she was like a ghost, centuries before the phenomena of being ghosted on your mobile was ever a thing. Being a ghost was both a curse and a blessing; she had freedom, she could wander anywhere without being seen, a street rat, scrabbling to grab and eat food that had fallen in the mud. Deaf to the world, but also with no voice, she had no family that she could ever remember. From the age of nine or ten she'd hovered on the edge of a small band of nomadic, cunning women, watching and learning from them; how to make food and medicines, what to eat, and as importantly, what not to eat. She was never a part of the company, or ever a part of anything, or anyone. Always on the edge, in that liminal space, not living, not dead, not connected, no fellowship, friends or family. As the years passed her eyesight faded. The world became a mist, and whilst walking along this grey road, soaked from the rain, she fell into the ditch and died.

It would be poetic to say she died at a crossroads; that would have made a tidy introduction to the liminal Goddess Hekate, guarding the crossroads, Propylaia, before the gate. I don't know if she transported my soul, and that is not how I remember when I first met her. Oh, yes, I should have said; the hobbled old woman was me, and I met myself through a regression hypnotherapy session. I guess like everyone else I imagined I was going to be a handmaiden to Cleopatra or the daughter of the Queen of Sheba, which would have made complete sense to me as my grandmother had always told me that we are direct descendants of her. However, it was not to be. I was a profoundly deaf beggar, who lost most of her sight but did at least learn a few things along the way to survive this miserable short life. I cried for days after the experience, but 30 years later I am glad, because reconnecting and reliving some of that tragic and miserable experience helped to make sense of my interests in the arcane and herbalism and in the inner and outer realms, the mind and a connection to what Jung would go on to call the collective unconscious and most importantly, being alone and living on the fringe. What I do know is that walking with Hekate is not an easy journey; it is demanding, certainties are stripped from you and the challenges that arise, even if overcome, should not be expected to reap rewards.

If that is your motivation for walking with a goddess, you would be better to choose someone who is more abundant in their provision for you.

I don't know if it's really a hangover from that life, but I am not very good at other people's clubs. Political, social, sports or organised religion leave me cold. I think back to that 'Aha' moment in Greek church, when a family enquired as to if I had an arrangement... safe with a rebel Greek Cypriot mum and English and bemused dad, fortunately for me (and the spare son) that was never going to happen. It's not just religious clubs, but also political ones. I did try. I was in the Labour Party Young Socialists, right up to the week before they were going to expel me, and whilst I can still confirm my tendencies are definitely to the left, I cannot imagine rejoining a party that removed clause IV from the back of their membership card.

Most people won't know the history of the Labour Party in the UK (and why should they!) Clause IV of the Labour Party's constitution was adopted in 1918 and originally committed the party to the 'common ownership of the means of production, distribution, and exchange.' This is the key foundation of a party committed to the fair distribution of wealth and investment in infrastructure that meant improving the quality of everyone's life.

In 1995, Tony Blair led a successful effort to amend Clause IV, removing the specific commitment to public ownership. For me, this was a turning point with the Labour Party moving from its socialist foundations to the social democratic movement it has become today. As with most of the clubs I have ever been involved with, I felt let down and quit.

Even in my long-time interest in the occult, there is not one group or movement or coven that has stirred me enough to seek acceptance, which has meant a lifetime of solitary practice. Before this all sounds too sad and tragic, just let me say that most people who know me experience me as gregarious and definitely 'at the party' if not always the life and soul. Don't get me wrong, I am not sitting in a little cottage alone on the edge of the woods tying kindling and selling herb bundles. My life is beautiful, with purpose through my work and my soulmate. We travel and work together, learn and create together. A fellow aquarian, Nat also tends to avoid other people's clubs.

Because of my lone practice, I felt I needed a guide, who would help with my development as a magician. I don't like practice that is not developed without some rigour underpinning the choices, but I found it difficult to find the right guide. Part of the struggle in choosing a guide is that very often they choose you, and it may not be clear why or how, but when you know, you know. Another challenge in making a conscious choice, is in understanding the many layers of a particular deity. The prism of history shines with many different hues, leaving it difficult to interpret and understand the real nature and energy you are working with. Goddesses like Hekate were transformed from powerful, multi-dimensional deities into 'dark' or 'evil' figures primarily through patriarchal restructuring of religious systems and narratives. This transformation reflects broader patterns of how society has historically dealt with powerful female figures.

Looking back in time, it is clearer how goddesses who operated independently of male control, especially those associated with wisdom, magic, and transformation, represented feminine power that existed outside patriarchal authority structures and which became something to be feared. In addition, patriarchal systems often establish strict binaries where qualities associated with masculinity (light, reason, order) are valued, while those associated with femininity (darkness, intuition, chaos) are demonised. As polytheistic traditions gave way to male-dominated monotheism and religious structures and processes, powerful goddesses were either absorbed as lesser figures, vilified, or recast as dangerous entities.

Finally, goddesses associated with herbal knowledge, healing, and reproductive wisdom represented women's autonomous knowledge systems that patriarchal institutions sought to control. Much in the same way that during the period of enlightenment, magic was cast into the waste bin of rejected knowledge, (Hanegraaff 2012) women-led magical practices were reduced to herbalism and medicine, and anything outside of this was often characterised as evil or wrong.

So, it is interesting in observing the rise and fall of the characteristics of Hekate, that it is not until the 20th century when more women were able to assert their rights and independence, that Hekate rises again and her following and veneration is possibly even more popular than ever. So, what is it that actually makes Hekate a dark, feminine deity? There are four main aspects; firstly, her association with night and darkness obviously any woman out after dark can't be up to any good, so she must be involved with necromancy and ghosts. Secondly, her knowledge of herbs and potions, which was associated with witchcraft and she as the mother of witches. Thirdly, Hekate's role in liminal spaces, being able to cross thresholds, and her association with the crossroads was reinterpreted as dangerous and transitional.

Finally, without a doubt, her independence from male deities was positioned as threatening rather than sovereign, as she did not have a rescuer, a lover or a male deity to whom she was beholden.

Obviously, my Cypriot heritage probably should have led me to Aphrodite, born of the foam on the shores in southwest Cyprus, but the fit was not right. This was partly because of her associations with love, fertility and marriage; they were not aspects of my womanhood and magickal practices that were most important to me. Whilst I do believe love is the most transformative magic available, I am not really a very 'peace, love and chocolate cake' person. I needed a goddess who would guide my thinking and work, and who would allow me to explore my whole nature, both the light and the dark.

I also wondered if Demeter would be the goddess that could guide and help me in my theurgic practice; there are certainly aspects of her mythos that resonate and appeal, not least the 'tiger mum' quality of being prepared to raze a planet to protect her daughter… but in the end, neither Demeter, nor any of the other traditional goddesses, resonated enough with the sort of work I was trying to undertake.

I can't honestly say I chose Hekate, and I don't really think it ever works quite like that. So, how I think I first met Hekate was in a transpersonal laboratory I had created. Let me just clarify, that is not bricks and mortar, but rather an aspect of Transpersonal Psychology, which emerged in the 1960s when researchers including Abraham Maslow and Stanislav Grof began studying experiences that transcend ordinary consciousness. Maslow explored peak experiences and self-transcendence beyond his hierarchy of needs in *Religions, Values, and Peak Experiences* (Maslow, 1964). Grof used psychedelic research to map non-ordinary states of consciousness (Grof, 1975). Roberto Assagioli made important contributions in his development of psychosynthesis which integrate spiritual dimensions into therapy (Assagioli, 1965). Ken Wilber later created integral theory to unite Eastern wisdom with Western psychology (Wilber, 1977). Since this time, there have been many other outstanding people that have contributed to this field, including Martha Crampton, but I digress.

The Transpersonal field offers practical tools for personal development by acknowledging that humans possess untapped potential beyond conventional psychology. The transpersonal house exercise demonstrates this approach.

Participants create an imaginary house, or lab, where different aspects of their psyche live as distinct characters. They visit rooms to dialogue with their inner critic, creative self, or wounded child. This technique helps people understand internal conflicts and integrate fragmented parts of themselves. Transpersonal psychology proves useful because it addresses the whole person, not just symptoms or behaviours. It recognises spiritual longing as natural rather than pathological. The approach helps people find meaning, purpose, and connection to something greater than themselves. This makes it valuable for those seeking growth beyond traditional therapeutic goals.

Nat and I have been interested in transpersonal work for a long time, and I had created a transpersonal house where I would work on issues, problems and conversations with the Self. My transpersonal house is actually quite modest, given it could have been a sumptuous castle, atop a hill or a super-modern bat cave buried in cliffs over the sea, which it isn't. I live in a solitary stone cottage. I never enter through the front door; always through the back, straight into the kitchen which is warm and inviting and where most conversations take place. Off the study (of course there is a study) there is a healing well that is replenished with waters from Aphrodite's bath place, (which incidentally you can visit, just north of Paphos in Cyprus). A few years after creating my transpersonal house, I experienced a traumatic and quite devastating health issue, which, not to be too dramatic, almost killed me. It has led to time in hospitals, operations and needing to use a wheelchair.

It was during this period I added to my transpersonal house by creating a transpersonal lab. Its function is to be a place where I can work out how to fix medical things, mind and body. I call it my 'vaulted lab' looks like an old alchemist's lab; there is a round brick wall that houses the furnace, with an alembic on top. Scattered around are broken things that each represent a non-functioning part of my body... I still haven't figured out what the old broken wooden pinball machine represents, but apart from being well worn, it's missing the spring. The first time I visited the lab, I entered, and was alone, although it was apparent that work was going on. I caught sight of a beautiful women with green eyes, walking down a wooden staircase toward me; it was Hekate. I instantly knew who she was, even if she did not fit the many descriptions available. As I reached the bottom of the staircase, she had disappeared. Instead, I was met by a sandy-haired man.

I have never seen his face; I am not sure he even has one, but if he does, I think it is freckled. He was a very grumpy short man; he wears a waxed apron and is always gruff and rude to me. I came to know him as the timekeeper. He laughed at me and said: 'Your first lesson is don't assume that what you see is what you see. You have work to do, so get on with it.' I felt stupid, at certainly taken down a peg or two. At that time, I knew little of Hekate, and the bits I did know seemed quite contradictory, so my own research began.

My own system for working with Hekate is described in detail in the final chapter. It is based on two dimensions, the first axis of what I call 'dirt to divine', which is a metaphorical ladder of development that reaches from the ground to the cosmos. It takes in a wide range of magical practices, starting with green magic, which I think is often (wrongly) considered to be the most basic form of magickal practice. Very often, it is associated more with folklore, wise old women and medicine rather than magickal practice in its own right. It's not as sexy as high ceremonial magic and is probably practiced more by women than men, I don't know about you, but I have never seen a picture of Aleister Crowley with a trowel. The second axis is that of 'internal' to 'external'.

This is the space where we move from our own internal landscape, thoughts ideas and dreams to the external manifestations and the material. But before we get into any one particular system, I want to begin with different aspects of my own journey that led me to develop this particular system of categorising what I do.

JOURNEYS THROUGH LIMINAL SPACE

You have probably already seen the various spellings of Hekate, Hecate, Hekaté. The original Greek form of the name appears as Ἑκάτη (with the rough breathing mark at the beginning and accent on the second syllable). This presents immediate challenges for translation into the Latin alphabet, as Greek contains sounds and accent marks without direct English equivalents. 'Hekate' represents the most direct translation, and follows modern conventions, with the initial 'H' representing the Greek rough breathing mark (indicating aspiration) and 'k' corresponding to the Greek kappa (κ). This form has gained particular favour among contemporary scholars and practitioners who seek fidelity to the original Greek pronunciation. 'Hecate', with its use of 'c' instead of 'k', reflects the Latinised form of the name that became standard in Classical Latin texts and subsequently dominated Western European literature for centuries. The Romans regularly changed the Greek kappa as 'c', which initially maintained the hard 'k' sound in Latin pronunciation.

This spelling gained currency through its use in influential works like Ovid's *Metamorphoses* and Virgil's *Aeneid*, and remains common in literary and popular contexts today.

Hekaté (or Hekátē represents a scholarly attempt to indicate the original Greek accentuation pattern. The acute accent over the 'a' or 'e' signals to readers that the stress falls on that syllable, guiding proper pronunciation. This form appears frequently in academic literature, particularly works focusing on Greek religion or Neoplatonism, where precision in representing the original pronunciation holds importance.

The contemporary preference for 'Hekate' over Hecate reflects broader shifts in classical transliteration practices. Throughout the 20th century, scholarly conventions increasingly favoured conversions that more accurately represented Greek rather than following Latinised forms. Meanwhile, literary and popular cultural references often retain the more familiar 'Hecate', the form most readers would recognise from Shakespeare's *Macbeth*, and countless other Western literary works.

Timeline

The earliest known references to Hekate in literature can be traced back to the 8th or 7th century BCE. Instead of 'Before Common Era' I use BCE to mean 'Before Christmas Even', which was once said to me by my driver in Iraq when he as describing the ancient citadel in Erbil. The citadel is one of the oldest continuously inhabited sites in the world.

Erbil was recorded in pre-Sumerian times, originally known in Aramaic as 'Arbela', and was an important political and religious centre. According to UNESCO, excavations reveal that life in the citadel preceded even these records and is estimated to been inhabited for at least 7,000 years. Anyway, Before Christmas Even, is, to me at least, a more emphatic description of history that these days we readily take for granted the millennia that have passed and the knowledge, rituals and practices that have continued to exist in one form or another.

My quest in understanding the contradictions about Hekate began with examining the timeline of knowledge and contributions to the many pieces of information that lead us to the current view of Hekate. Attempting to bring together any form of timeline to describe the emergence and veneration of Hekate is the basis for a complete book in its own right. What I aim to achieve here is to highlight what I believe to be some of the key sources and trends in Hekate's known and seen influence. I declare my interest, bias and therefore scope being the areas that I actually know something about, link back to my own ancestors and heritage and consequently hold an interest for me. These are primarily in Cyprus and Greece, from where I am culturally descended and Italy, my chosen home.

However, before diving into a possible timeline, it is worth considering two very different schools of thought about Hekate. The first is the manifestations of Hekate that derive from what is ostensibly the Greek traditions and expanded to reflect different aspects of the goddess in her different forms. The second derives from the Cosmic World Soul philosophy as characterised in the *Chaldean Oracles*.

There is an argument that Hekate is of Anatolian origins, in the form of the Carian goddess, also known Hekate and indeed, the oldest known temple dedicated to Hekate was discovered in Lagina, Caria (which is in modern-day Turkey), dating around the 6th century BCE. This sacred site remained an important centre of her worship well into the Roman period. Caria occupied a strategic position in ancient Anatolia bordered by Lydia to the north, Phrygia to the east, and the Aegean Sea to the west. Major Carian cities including Halicarnassus, Mylasa, and Lagina became important centres of Hekate worship. However, it is also thought that Hekate was, at the same time, venerated in parts of Greece.

The Chaldean Oracles
The origins of the *Chaldean Oracles* are unclear, as generally they are doctrines that were handed down orally.

They are most often, although probably incorrectly attributed, to Julian the Theurgist and/or his father, Julian the Chaldean. The term Chaldean may indicate either that he was from Chaldea, or signify that he was a magician, astronomer or practitioner of 'mysterious arts'. These 'arts' were generally passed from father to son, which would explain some of the ambiguity relating to attribution. Chaldea is the classical Greek term for Babylon, which referred to an area southeast of Babylonia near the Persian Gulf, covering what today would be considered Southern Iraq but also extending across most of Syria and parts of Jordan and Israel. There is no physical Chaldean oracle to speak of, that could be understood like the ancient Greek Oracle at Delphi. The *Chaldean Oracles* apparently derived from verses spoken whilst Julian was in a trance state, which always makes me think of Helene Blavatsky's description of how her two-volume book *Isis Unveiled* was produced. What exists of the *Chaldean Oracles* today are fragments reconstructed or curated by Neoplatonist and Christian philosophers. Neoplatonists including Porphyry, Iamblichus, and Proclus wrote extensive commentaries on the Oracles, with the most extensive surviving commentary written by the Christian philosopher Michael Psellos in the 11th century.

The idea of Hekate as the Cosmic World Soul in the *Chaldean Oracles* significantly differs from earlier Greek magickal and religious traditions. The concept of the World Soul mainly originates from Platonic philosophy. In Timaeus, Plato (it always goes back to the Greeks) describes the World Soul as an intermediary principle between the realm of Forms and the material world, responsible for implementing divine order in the cosmos. This philosophical framework provided the theoretical foundation for Hekate's cosmic status. The Platonic World Soul has several crucial functions: it acts as a mediating principle between the 'intelligible' and 'sensible' realms and provides animation and order to the material cosmos. Central to this is the role of implementing divine intelligence in the physical world and maintaining cosmic harmony.

One of the most distinctive characterisations of Hekaté-Physis in the Oracles is her description as a 'membrane' (ὑμήν) between worlds. Fragment 38 (preserved by Psellos) states:

'[The Father] measured and marked out all things with the membrane [ὑμήν] of Hekaté placed in the middle.'

This portrayal suggests that Hekaté-Physis forms the boundary, or interface, between the intelligible and sensible realms.

As the Cosmic World Soul, Hekate is the intermediary between the highest divine realms and the material world. This role builds on her traditional association with boundaries and crossing points but elevates it to cosmic significance. She becomes responsible for transmitting divine ideas into material manifestation, acting as both a generative and ordering power. The Oracles present Hekate as the source of life-giving power, emphasising her role in animating and giving vitality to the cosmos. She becomes responsible not just for biological life, but for all forms of cosmic animation and activity. The metaphysical structure presented in the *Chaldean Oracles* places Hekate in an important position within a hierarchical cosmos. Above her lies the realm of pure intellect, associated with the highest divine principles. Below her extends the material world in all its complexity. As World Soul, Hekate serves as the essential link between these realms, ensuring the transmission of divine order into material being.

This positioning resolves a fundamental philosophical problem: how does pure, immaterial intellect interact with and influence the material world? Hekate as World Soul provides the necessary mediating principle, capable of receiving pure intellectual forms and implementing them in material reality.

The Sola Busca tarot illustrates Hekaté as Physis in the Four of Discs (or Coins), revealing direct links from late medieval Italian esotericism and the Neoplatonic traditions that preserved ancient conceptions of Hekate. Created around 1490 in northern Italy, the Sola Busca tarot diverges significantly from standard tarot iconography of its era. Unlike contemporary decks, it features fully-illustrated cards with elaborate scenes depicting historical, mythological and allegorical figures. The deck is replete with hermetic and alchemical symbolism. The Four of Discs is a compelling image associated with Hekaté in her aspect as Physis, or Nature. The card depicts a naked female figure, with pubic hair, which in itself was very unusual for the period. Peter Mark Adams (2017). She reflects the profound influence of Neoplatonic philosophy on Renaissance esotericism. Platonic texts had reintroduced these concepts to Italian intellectual circles in the decades preceding the deck's creation.

The Neoplatonic conception of Hekaté as the universal matrix through which divine ideas manifest into material form aligns perfectly with her positioning in the Four of Discs the number four traditionally associated with materiality and physical manifestation. The iconographic details on the card, particularly the four discs arranged in a pattern suggestive of cosmic order echo Proclus's description of Hekaté as governing the 'tetrad of the elements' and the 'quarters of the world'. This conception presents Hekaté not merely as a goddess of magic and liminality, but as the very principle of ordered manifestation underlying the material cosmos. The presence of Hekaté Physis in the Four of Discs also reflects the deck's likely use in Renaissance magical practices. The Sola Busca was not merely a game or divinatory tool, but appears designed as what Renaissance magi would term an 'ensouled image'; a material object constructed according to astrological and symbolic principles to attract specific celestial influences.

From the Iron Age and the Golden Age: 800 BCE – 300 BCE
Pre-7th Century BCE, the archaeological evidence from western Anatolia identifies a goddess with characteristics later associated with Hekate, particularly in Caria.

The name 'Hekate' possibly derives from the Carian language rather than Greek, although the root word Hekat is also the basis of both the Egyptian word for magic and the Heqet is the Egyptian goddess of fertility and life bearer, the goddess of creation, midwifery, and the germination of barley, who has a human figure with a frog head. Heqet was known of from around 2890 BC. Evidence from Caria, particularly from the sanctuary at Lagina, suggests Hekate functioned as a main deity with broad domains rather than the more specialised figure she became in Greek observances. The Carian Hekate appears as a state goddess with strong territorial and civic aspects, and as a goddess integrated into public and civic religion, with festivals (Hekatesia) that included athletic competitions and public processions, suggesting a deity central to communal identity rather than operating primarily in liminal or magical contexts.

The first known written reference to Hekate appears in Hesiod's *Theogony* (circa 700 BCE), which is more or less contemporary with the temples at Lagina, where she is described as a powerful pre-Olympian goddess honoured by Zeus. Hesiod describes her as a universal goddess who holds sway over earth, sea, and sky, granted 'splendid gifts' and a share in all three realms.

Theogony is a 1000-line poem that recounts both the birth of the pantheon of Greek goddesses and gods, as well as cosmology and the beginning of the world. According to Hesiod's detailed family tree, Phoebe, a daughter of Uranus and Ge, was the mother (and Coeus the father) of Asteria and Leto. Hekate is the daughter of Asteria and Perses. Although it is also argued that she is in fact a daughter of Zeus and Demeter. Regardless of the origin, it is clear from Hesiod that Hekate had a strong bond with Zeus and the Olympians and was favoured by Zeus who: 'Honoured her above all. He gave her splendid gifts to have a share of the earth and unfruitful sea.' Hekate had dominion in the sky, on the earth and in the sea. Hesiod went on to say of Hekate that she is:

'...honoured exceedingly by the deathless gods. For to this day, whenever anyone of men on earth offers rich sacrifices and prays for favour according to custom, he calls upon Hecate. Great honour comes full easily to him whose prayers the goddess receives favourably, and she bestows wealth upon him; for the power surely is with her.'

It is less reported that Zeus also bestowed upon Hekate a role as 'a nurse of the young who after that day saw with their eyes the light of all-seeing Dawn.'

This accolade of the 'Light of all-seeing Dawn' may also be a source of the connection between Hekate and Ēastre. It is interesting because by the middle of the fifth century, when Euripides was producing Medea, Hekate is no longer regarded as the goddess that nurses the young, but revered as the deity connected to ghosts, witchcraft, and sorcery who would do harm to pregnant women or newborn infants. So somewhere in history, the perception of Hekate changed dramatically, and when I say dramatically, I don't just mean substantially, I also mean in a literal sense, through the eyes of the playwrights, including Shakespeare, who much later, reflected a new image and voice of Hekate. Archaeological findings reveal that by the 6th and 5th Century BCE, Hekate worship spread throughout Greece, especially in Athens, but also into the area called by the Romans Magna Graecia (greater Greece). This expansion included Italy, and in particular Sicily. The site of Selinunte was an important settlement on the southwest coast of Sicily. The acropolis of Selinunte was situated between two rivers, consisting of five temples, the largest being a temple dedicated to Demeter, where votive offerings to Persephone, Hekate and Demeter have been found. These three goddesses are central to the Eleusinian Mysteries and Persephone's abduction took place in Locri Sicily. In 680 BCE, Locri was founded.

In 680 BCE Locri was a Greek colony of Magna Graecia, located in the Calabria region of southern Italy. Locri was the site of an important sanctuary to Persephone, and votives unearthed at this site portray Persephone as the 'Queen of the Dead', next to Hades. Included in the many votives, plaques, and other artifacts found at the site, is a considerable number of offerings to Hekate.

An interesting archaeological find was discovered within Persephone's temple – a plaque of a winged female daimon; the winged messenger/angelic chthonic deity who is identified with both Hekate and Artemis. Winged deities who travel between the worlds are typically psychopomps guiding or transporting dead and departed souls, of which we will hear more later.

The Homeric Hymn to Demeter charts Hekate's journeys, where she witnesses Persephone enter the Underworld, and then welcomes her back when she returns. Hekate's chthonic nature is further propagated by contemporary vase paintings which depict Hekate with torches accompanying Persephone between the living and the dead. In this period, Hekate was frequently depicted in Greek art and featured in plays.

During the 4th century BCE, Hekate was incorporated into the Eleusinian Mysteries. The chronicle of Demeter and her search of Persephone is the foundation of the Eleusinian, mysteries and it is Hekate who emerges as the critical intermediary. When Persephone was abducted by Hades, Hekate was the only deity who heard her initial cries. She then became Demeter's companion during her desperate search, carrying torches to illuminate the dark path. The sacred ceremonies were dedicated to Demeter and Persephone, focusing on a narrative of divine loss, search, and eventual reunion that symbolised the cycles of life, death and rebirth. Interestingly, participation was remarkably inclusive, with the rites being open to any Greek-speaking individual who had not committed murder.

The most sacred moments of the rites involved symbolic representations of death and rebirth. Participants would metaphorically descend into underworld realms, confronting existential fears and emerging with renewed understanding. This was not a passive experience but an active, participatory journey of personal and collective transformation. The Mysteries involved elaborate ceremonies that were strictly confidential. Initiates were sworn to absolute secrecy, a vow maintained with remarkable consistency.

The core experience involved re-enactments of the Demeter-Persephone chronicle, along with ritualistic representations of death and rebirth, the use of psychoactive substances to induce transcendent experiences, which were probably based on the hallucinogenic qualities of ergot, and the symbolic journeys through darkness towards enlightenment.

The Mysteries were divided into two primary phases. The Lesser Mysteries were a pathway of preparation and marked the initial stage of a profound spiritual journey. Conducted during the spring months, these preliminary rituals served as a critical gateway for potential initiates. The initiates would arrive at the Agrai sanctuary, their bodies and spirits prepared for a transformative experience. The purification process was both physical and metaphysical. Initiates would first undergo ritual bathing in sacred streams, symbolically washing away mundane impurities. Priests and priestesses guided them through intricate cleansing ceremonies, each movement and action laden with deep spiritual significance. Sacrificial offerings to Demeter and Persephone accompanied these rituals, establishing a sacred covenant between the human and divine realms. Initiates would change into specially prepared garments, each fabric and fold representing spiritual layers being shed and renewed.

Lectures and oral traditions introduced participants to the fundamental mythological narratives, providing contextual understanding for the deeper mysteries to come.

The Greater Mysteries were a transformative celebration. As autumn approached, the most sacred phase of the Eleusinian Mysteries would begin. The procession would wind its way from Athens to Eleusis, participants carrying sacred ritual objects and creating a living, moving testament to spiritual devotion. Rhythmic chants and ancient musical traditions accompanied the journey, building collective anticipation and spiritual energy. The Telesterion Hall was a sacred space designed to contain the most profound spiritual revelations. Here, initiates would experience a re-enactment of the Demeter-Persephone story. The performance was not merely theatrical but a deeply immersive spiritual experience, allowing participants to psychologically and emotionally connect with the cycles of loss, search, and reunion. Hekate's torches were important to these rituals, representing the transition from ignorance to understanding. Initiates would have seen her as a spiritual guide, illuminating the path between different states of consciousness. Central to the ceremony was the consumption of kykeon, which is described as either a breakfast drink or a sacred ritualistic libation.

The inclusion of barley in most of the kykeon recipes has led researchers to conclude that ergot fungus (Claviceps purpurea) could have been the cause of hallucinations and altered states of consciousness associated with ergot poisoning, known as ergotism. Ergot contains alkaloids that can cause severe physiological effects, including hallucinations, muscle spasms, gangrene and potentially fatal poisoning. While the extent of ergot's presence and impact in ancient Greek society is still a matter of debate, archaeological and botanical evidence confirms that the fungus existed in the region during that historical period. In Homeric works, kykeon is described in at least three different ways: in the *Iliad*, the *Odyssey* and the *Hymn to Demeter*. In the *Iliad*,

'....the woman, as fair as a goddess, mixed them a mess with Pramnian wine; she grated goat's milk cheese into it with a bronze grater, threw in a handful of white barley-meal, and having thus prepared the mess she bade them drink it.'

However, in the *Odyssey*, it is described that,

'[Circe] brought them in and made them sit on chairs and seats and made for them a portion of cheese and barley meal and yellow honey with Pramnian wine; but in the food she mixed baneful drugs, that they might utterly forget their native land.'

And finally, the *Hymn to Demeter*, tells that,

> '*Metaneira offered [Demeter] a cup, having filled it with honey-sweet wine. But she refused, saying that it was divinely ordained that she does not drink red wine. Then [Demeter] ordered [Metaneira] to mix some barley and water with delicate pennyroyal, and to give [Demeter] that potion to drink. So [Metaneira] made the kykeôn and offered it to the goddess, just as she had ordered.*'

The Eleusinian Mysteries maintained their significance for nearly two thousand years, from approximately 1600 BCE to 392 CE. Archaeological evidence from Eleusis reveals aspects of Hekate's role as a psychopomp, guiding initiates through the liminal spaces between known and unknown, life and death, ignorance and enlightenment.

The Classical Age From 300–100 BCE
During the 3rd century BCE, Hekate's influence expanded in Egypt, coinciding with the Ptolemaic period, when Greek and Egyptian cultures were increasingly intermingling. This growth likely stemmed from the Ptolemaic dynasty's deliberate efforts to blend Greek and Egyptian religious traditions. Throughout the Mediterranean basin, from the 3rd to 1st centuries BCE, Hekate worship underwent a remarkable expansion.

This period witnessed the goddess's evolution from her earlier Greek origins, and her associations with the crossroads, liminal spaces and magic much stronger. Her worship spread beyond traditional Greek territories, through trade routes and cultural exchange.

Hekate's integration into Egyptian magickal traditions centred around Isis and Thoth, where there are compelling parallels. In Ptolemaic Egypt, Hekate became associated with Isis in her magical aspects, particularly in relation to knowledge of herbs and poisonous plants. She links to Thoth through shared connections to magical knowledge and liminal spaces. The Egyptian magical traditions incorporated Hekate into their practice through hymns and spells that merged Greek and Egyptian elements. She was often invoked in Egyptian magic for protection, particularly against malevolent spirits and harmful magic. Her triple-formed nature resonated with Egyptian concepts of divine multiplicities, and she was sometimes depicted in Egyptian magical contexts with attributes of both Greek and Egyptian deities.

The transition into the Roman period, beginning in the 1st century BCE, saw Hekate's worship undergo further transformation. The Romans, known for their ability to absorb and adapt foreign deities, incorporated Hekate into their religious traditions.

This assimilation continued through the 4th century CE, with Hekate maintaining her associations with magic, crossroads, and the supernatural whilst gaining new dimensions within Roman religious practice.

The Roman adoption of Hekate as a goddess was complex and multifaceted. The Romans initially encountered her through their contact with Greek colonies in southern Italy, where she was already well-established. As Rome expanded, Hekate's worship was officially recognised and she became associated with the Roman goddess Trivia, who presided over crossroads. This association strengthened her connection to liminal spaces in Roman religious thought.

In Roman religious practice, Hekate maintained her Greek associations with magic and crossroads but was also incorporated into household worship. Small shrines to Hekate, known as Hecataea were commonly placed at crossroads and doorways throughout Roman cities. She became particularly popular among Roman women, who would leave offerings at these shrines for protection and blessing. The Romans also emphasised her role as a guardian of doorways and transitions, making her an important deity in both public and private religious practice.

After Constantine's conversion and the subsequent Christianisation of the Roman Empire, traditional pagan practices faced increasing suppression. During this period, the worship of Hekate underwent significant changes. But whilst her temples and public shrines were often destroyed or converted to Christian use, her influence persisted in more subtle ways.

The Theodosian Code was a compilation of the laws of the Roman Empire under the Christian emperors (312 CE). This and other imperial edicts gradually restricted pagan practices, forcing devotees to practise their traditions in increasingly private settings. However, some aspects of Hekate's worship remained remarkably resilient, particularly in rural areas and amongst those who maintained magical practices.Hekate's prominence in magical practices during the 2nd and 3rd centuries CE is evidenced by the Greek Magical Papyri (PGM). These texts, discovered in Egypt, reveal the sophisticated magical traditions that had developed around her worship. They contain spells, hymns, and rituals that demonstrate how Hekate had become a central figure in the magical practices of the Roman Empire, bridging Greek, Egyptian, and Roman magical traditions. The PGM provide some of the richest evidence for Hekate's role in magical practice during this period.

These texts were primarily written in Greek and Demotic and reveal Hekate as a powerful goddess of magic who could be invoked for various purposes, from love spells to curse tablets. In the PGM texts Hekate is often described with elaborate magical names and titles, reflecting her immense power in magical practice.

She is frequently invoked as 'three-formed' or 'triple-headed' Hekate, and the papyri provide detailed instructions for rituals dedicated to her. These include specific times for invocation (often at night or at crossroads), particular offerings (including garlic, eggs, and dark-coloured animals), and the nature of the ceremonial procedures. The papyri reveal Hekate's role as a mediator between the mortal and divine realms. She was often called upon to facilitate communication with other deities or spirits, and her aid was sought in necromantic rituals. Particularly interesting are the hymns to Hekate found in the papyri, which reveal her as a cosmic deity with power over heaven, earth, and the underworld. These hymns often describe her in terrifying terms, emphasising her control over ghosts and her ability to bring forth supernatural entities. The papyri also contain detailed descriptions of how to create phylacteries (small leather boxes that contained texts) and amulets dedicated to Hekate for protection and power.

Late Antiquity and Early Middle Ages (3rd – 7th Centuries CE)

The perception and worship of Hekate underwent significant transformations during Late Antiquity (3rd–7th centuries CE) and into the Early Middle Ages. The rise of Christianity and vigour to convert to a monotheistic world view played a significant role in this.

At the beginning of this period, in the *Hymn to the Mother of the Gods*, written by Emperor Julian (331–363 CE), Hekate is described as one of the primary divine powers, specifically associating her with both cosmic and earthly boundaries. Julian's personal devotion to Hekate is further evidenced by his practice of making offerings at crossroads during his military campaigns. Christian theologian Clement of Alexandria (c. 150–215 CE) discusses Hekate in his *Protrepticus,* describing specific ritual practices that were still current during his time, including the maintenance of household shrines and the leaving of offerings at crossroads. The writings of Nonnus (5th century CE) in his *Dionysiaca* present Hekate in a complex light, incorporating both traditional and newer associations. He specifically describes her as 'three-headed Hekate, who shoots forth terrible rays from her forehead,' providing evidence for the continuing development of her iconography in Late Antiquity.

The writings of Olympiodorus the younger, (c. 495–570 CE) demonstrate the continuing philosophical interest in Hekate within Neoplatonic circles. His commentary on Plato's Alcibiades specifically discusses Hekate's role as a mediating deity between the intellectual and material realms, providing evidence for the sophisticated theological interpretations of her nature that persisted in philosophical circles.

The *Chaldean Oracles*, probably composed in the late 2nd or early 3rd century CE but extensively commented upon throughout Late Antiquity, present Hekate in an elevated position. In these texts, she is the Cosmic Soul and intermediary between the divine and material realms. Proclus (412-485 CE), in his *Commentary on the Chaldean Oracles*, provides specific details about how this conception of Hekate was understood, describing her as the 'life-giving goddess' who 'fills all things with intellectual light'.

Damascius (c. 458–538 CE), in his *Problems and Solutions Concerning First Principles*, discusses Hekate's role in Neoplatonic theology. He specifically describes her as maintaining the bonds between the material and divine worlds, providing a philosophical interpretation of her traditional association with crossroads and boundaries.

Evidence of continued active worship of the Hellenistic deities was recorded by John of Ephesus, a sixth century bishop, historian and theologian, who documented. The destruction of pagan shrines in his missionary work on Asia Minor and its shrines. His accounts, although hostile, illustrate the continuing ritual practices, including nocturnal gatherings and offerings at crossroads. These practices were still common enough to warrant legislative attention such as *The Theodosian Code* (438 CE) which specifically prohibits certain practices associated with the worship of Hekate, including leaving offerings at crossroads and maintaining household shrines. The gradual decline of public worship is evidenced by the archaeological record, which shows the abandonment or destruction of many temples and shrines during the 5th and 6th centuries CE. However, the discovery of private devotional objects from this period suggests the continuation of personal worship practices.

Archaeological evidence from this period includes several significant finds from Alexandria. A 4th-century CE temple complex contained multiple representations of Hekate, alongside ritual implements. The partially-preserved temple inventory lists specific items used in her worship: bronze torches, specially crafted keys, and vessels marked with triple-formed imagery. Evidence from the late 4th century CE shows the continuing practice of leaving offerings at crossroads, though now often in a syncretic context.

An inscription from Aphrodisias, dated to approximately 380 CE, mentions 'offerings to Hekate-Selene at the triple crossroads', indicating the merger of Hekate with lunar deities that became increasingly common in this period. Findings from Ephesus include amulets and small shrines dating to this period, often showing Hekate alongside Christian symbols, indicating the complex processes of religious transformation. Similar findings from Athens show the continuation of Hekate's worship into the 5th century CE. The discovery of a shrine near the Agora, dated approximately 420 CE, contained multiple votive offerings including clay dogs and miniature torches. The shrine's destruction layer, dated to the late 5th century, provides evidence of the gradual suppression of pagan practices. The magical tradition associated with Hekate continued to develop during this period, as evidenced by numerous curse tablets and magical gems. A particularly well-preserved example from 4th-century CE Cyprus shows Hekate in her triple form surrounded by magical characters and voces mysticae, demonstrating the integration of her traditional imagery with newer magical practices.

The archaeological record from Constantinople provides evidence of the survival of Hekate's worship in the imperial capital into the 6th century CE. Excavations near the Hippodrome revealed a small shrine containing triple-formed Hekate images alongside Christian symbols, suggesting the complex religious environment of the period. The gradual transformation of Hekate's image during this period is evidenced by changes in artistic representations. Late antique gems and amulets increasingly show her merged with other deities, particularly Artemis and Selene, creating complex syncretic images that reflect the religious developments of the period. The magical papyri from this period provide detailed evidence of how Hekate was invoked in protective magic. A 6th-century CE text from Egypt provides specific instructions for creating protective amulets bearing Hekate's image, demonstrating the persistence of magical practices associated with her.

The survival of Hekate in magical traditions is particularly evident in the numerous magical handbooks and formularies that continued to be copied and transmitted throughout this period.

These texts preserve specific invocations and ritual practices, demonstrating the persistence of magical traditions associated with Hekate even as public worship declined.

The archaeological and textual evidence from this period reveals a complex process of transformation and adaptation in the worship and perception of Hekate. While public cult practices gradually declined under Christian pressure, elements of her worship survived in philosophical interpretations, magical practices, and syncretic forms. The period saw both the sophisticated theological developments of Neoplatonic philosophy and the continuation of traditional practical worship, particularly in private and magical contexts.

The magical papyri from Late Antique Egypt provide detailed evidence of how Hekate was invoked in magical practices. The Greek Magical Papyri (PGM IV, 3rd–4th centuries CE) contains specific invocations to Hekate, including detailed ritual instructions. One particularly well-preserved example prescribes: 'Take a lamp not coloured red, dress it with clean linen, and in the first hour of the night bring it to a crossroads. Draw a circle with sulphur and place the lamp in the middle. Recite the following invocation to Hekate seven times...'

This suggests that rather than a simple decline, the Late Antique and Early Medieval period saw a complex transformation of Hekate's role and significance, with different aspects of her worship and mythology surviving and adapting in various ways across different contexts and regions.

The Middle Ages to the Early Modern Period (11th–17th centuries CE)

The Middle Ages through to the Early Modern Period (11th–17th centuries CE) saw Hekate's presence diminish in mainstream culture. In most of Europe, knowledge of her became largely confined to scholarly works and classical literature. However, she maintained a presence in occult traditions, where she was often portrayed as a powerful figure in ceremonial magic.

Medieval and Renaissance grimoires sometimes included invocations to Hekate, though these were often heavily modified from their classical origins. The preservation of Hekate in occult traditions helped preserve knowledge of her until the revival of interest in classical paganism during the Renaissance and later periods. During the medieval and early modern periods, Hekate's presence in grimoires and magical texts underwent several transformations. In many cases, she appeared under various pseudonyms and alternative titles, often carefully worded to avoid ecclesiastical censure.

In medieval grimoires, particularly those from the 13th–15th centuries, references to Hekate were sometimes disguised using Hebrew or Aramaic names, presenting her as an angel or spiritual force rather than a goddess. Some texts referred to her as 'Regina Nocturna' (Queen of the Night) or incorporated her attributes into descriptions of other spiritual entities. The *Key of Solomon*, whilst not explicitly naming Hekate, contains several rituals and magical operations that bear striking similarities to classical ceremonies associated with her worship. The *Picatrix*, a medieval grimoire of Arabic origin, that was later translated into Latin, contains several references to planetary spirits and magical practices that scholars have linked to classical Hekate worship, though under different names. The text's descriptions of nocturnal rituals at crossroads and certain magical preparations bear remarkable similarities to ancient Hekate rites.

The Christianisation of Hekate's attributes in these texts often manifested in complex ways. Some grimoires presented her as a powerful spirit who could be commanded through Christian prayers and invocations, whilst others transformed her into an angel who had knowledge of crossroads magic and necromancy. In some cases, her triple-formed nature was reinterpreted through Christian trinitarian concepts, making her more acceptable to Christian practitioners of ceremonial magic.

In Mediterranean magical traditions, particularly in Italian and Greek texts, references to Hekate sometimes survived under the guise of various saints or spiritual entities associated with magic and crossroads. These texts often preserved more direct links to classical traditions, though still heavily modified to fit Christian theological frameworks. In Mediterranean magical traditions, particularly during the medieval and early modern periods, the survival of Hekate through saintly associations presents a fascinating example of religious syncretism.
In Greek territories, especially in rural areas and islands where ancient traditions persisted Hekate's attributes were often transferred to various Orthodox saints.

In Italian magical traditions, particularly in southern Italy where Greek influence remained strong, Hekate's characteristics were often absorbed into the veneration of various female saints.

In terms of Italian practices, the Madonna Della Strada (Our Lady of the Way) in Italian tradition absorbed some aspects of Hekate's role as a protector of travellers and crossroads. Local traditions would sometimes incorporate invocations to her that bore striking similarities to ancient Hekate prayers, particularly in their emphasis on protection during night-time travel.

Certain magical practices involving crossroads, particularly those performed at night or during liminal times like dawn or dusk, preserved elements of ancient Hekate worship whilst outwardly conforming to Christian practice. These parallels with Hekate emerge in several interesting ways. Like Hekate Enodia (Hekate of the Ways), Madonna Della Strada was invoked for protection during travel.

In some Italian regions, particularly in the south, traditional offerings to Madonna Della Strada were sometimes left at crossroads – a practice remarkably similar to the ancient custom of leaving Deipnon (Hekate's supper) at crossroads.

In some German magical texts from the 15th and 16th centuries, aspects of Hekate appear in descriptions of Frau Holda and Perchta, supernatural figures associated with crossroads and night-time gatherings.

These figures, whilst not explicitly identified as Hekate, share many of her traditional attributes and magical associations.

The *Munich Manual of Demonic Magic*, a 15th-century grimoire, contains ceremonies that parallel ancient Hekate rituals, particularly in its instructions for crossroads magic and necromantic operations. Though Hekate isn't named directly, the procedures and timing of certain rituals strongly suggest her influence. The alteration in Hekate's portrayal can be partially attributed to the medieval Christian interpretation of classical deities.

The 13th-century text *De deorum imaginibus libellus* describes Hekate primarily in terms of her association with magic and the underworld, omitting many of her protective and beneficial aspects that were prominent in classical sources. The reasons for these transformations in Hekate's image are complex. The medieval period's general tendency to recast pagan deities as demons or malevolent spirits played a significant role. Additionally, the period's preoccupation with witchcraft likely influenced the emphasis on Hekate's more sinister aspects.

The medieval grimoire tradition provides interesting insight into how magical practitioners of the period viewed Hekate.

The *Munich Manual of Demonic Magic*, although not referring directly to Hekate, does focus on demonology and necromancy contains several invocations with invocations of beings such as Satan, Lilith, Astaroth and Samael, thus suggesting the survival of some classical elements in magical practice, though often heavily modified by Christian and medieval magical concepts.

The period's scholarly works often attempted to systematise understanding of classical deities. Natale Conti's *Mythologiae* (1567) presents Hekate in a way that tries to reconcile classical sources with contemporary interpretations, though still emphasising supernatural and magical aspects. What's particularly interesting is how selective this transformation was. Classical sources certainly associated Hekate with magic and the underworld, but these were just aspects of a much more complex divine figure. Medieval and Renaissance sources often amplified these elements while minimising or ignoring others. The influence of Ovid's *Metamorphoses*, particularly through Arthur Golding's 1567 English translation, significantly shaped Renaissance understanding of classical deities. Ovid's brief mentions of Hekate, particularly in connection with Medea's magical practices, likely influenced later artistic representations.

The limited access to classical sources meant that medieval and Renaissance understanding of Hekate was often based on selective or incomplete readings of ancient texts.

As a consequence, the Medieval and Renaissance transformation of Hekate represents a significant move from the classical understanding.

Where ancient sources presented a complex deity with various spheres of influence, and both beneficial and dangerous aspects, Medieval and Renaissance sources often reduced her to a more one-dimensional figure associated primarily with witchcraft and dark magic. This transformation reflects broader cultural changes: the shift from polytheism to Christianity, the development of new literary and artistic traditions, and changing social attitudes toward magic and the supernatural. As a consequence, Medieval and Renaissance Europe reinterpreted pagan deities, often casting them in negative roles, with more positive qualities being re-attributed to saints. The social and political context saw a dramatic rise in witch hunting and the witch trials. Between 1560 and 1670 there were more than 40,000 deaths, and this will most certainly have influenced how supernatural figures were portrayed in literature and art.

The Renaissance tendency to adapt classical material for contemporary audiences often led to significant modifications of original meanings and contexts. There are distinct geographical variations in how Hekate was understood. In areas with more humanist traditions, such as Italy, representations tended to show more awareness of classical sources, while in northern Europe, the association with witchcraft was often stronger.

By the 16th and 17th centuries, as interest in classical learning grew during the Renaissance, some magical texts began to reference Hekate more directly, though usually still within a Christianised context. These later grimoires often attempted to reconcile classical magical practices with Christian theology, presenting Hekate's powers as operating under divine authority rather than in opposition to it. The Medieval and Renaissance conception of Hekate differs markedly from classical representations, with Shakespeare's portrayal in *Macbeth* (c. 1606) serving as perhaps the most influential example. In Act III, Scene 5, Hekate appears as the queen of witches, chastising the three weird sisters:

'Have I not reason, beldams as you are, Saucy and overbold? How did you dare to trade and traffic with Macbeth in riddles and affairs of death...'

This portrayal represents a significant departure from classical representations. Where ancient sources often showed Hekate as a complex deity associated with crossroads, protection, and spiritual transition, Shakespeare presents her primarily as a malevolent figure associated with witchcraft and dark magic.

The transformation of Hekate's image began during the medieval period, influenced significantly by Christian interpretations of pagan deities. Reginald Scot's *The Discoverie of Witchcraft* (1584) provides insight into how Hekate was understood during this period. Scot describes her as 'the governess of the witches', though interestingly, he does so while arguing against the reality of witchcraft, suggesting the complexity of contemporary attitudes. The transformation of Hekate's image also reflects broader social anxieties of the period. The emphasis on her connection to witchcraft coincides with the height of witch hunts in Europe, suggesting that ancient deities were being recast to reflect contemporary concerns.

The association between Hekate and the moon, present in classical sources but not predominant, became increasingly emphasised during this period. This may reflect the Medieval and Renaissance preoccupation with astrological and lunar influences on earthly affairs. Edmund Spenser's *The Faerie Queene* (1589) presents a more nuanced view, occasionally referring to Hekate in her classical triple form and acknowledging her association with the moon. However, even here, the emphasis tends toward her darker aspects.

Ben Jonson's *The Masque of Queens* (1609) presents another significant literary portrayal of Hekate. In this work, she is depicted as the leader of a coven of witches, though Jonson's extensive scholarly footnotes demonstrate his awareness of classical sources. This suggests a conscious literary choice to emphasise certain aspects of Hekate's character over others. John Webster's *The Duchess of Malfi* (1614) makes reference to Hekate in a similarly dark context, associating her with poisoning and midnight rituals. This reflects the general trend in Renaissance literature to portray classical deities through a darker lens, often stripping away their more benevolent aspects. The medieval period's understanding of Hekate was also influenced by late classical sources, particularly the magical papyri and Neoplatonic texts. However, these complex theological and magical traditions were often simplified and reinterpreted through a Christian lens. Thomas Heywood's *The Hierarchie of the Blessed Angells* (1635) attempts to reconcile classical and contemporary views of Hekate, acknowledging her triple form and association with crossroads while still emphasising her connection to witchcraft. This work demonstrates the period's struggle to integrate classical learning with contemporary religious and social views.

Early Modern Period–The Romantic Revival: 18th–19th Century

The 18th and 19th centuries witnessed a significant revival of interest in ancient paganism, including Hekate, largely driven by the Romantic movement's fascination with classical antiquity. During this period, Hekate emerged from relative obscurity to become a compelling figure in both literary and occult circles in Britain and Europe. The Romantic poets, with their deep appreciation for mysticism and ancient wisdom, found in Hekate a powerful symbol of liminal spaces and forbidden knowledge. Percy Bysshe Shelley referenced her in his poetry, while writers like Johann Wolfgang von Goethe incorporated her into their works, most notably in *Faust*, where she appears as a powerful chthonic deity (Butler, 1998). This literary revival paralleled a growing scholarly interest in ancient religions and mythology.

The late 19th century saw Hekate's significance increase substantially with the establishment of influential occult organisations. The Hermetic Order of the Golden Dawn, founded in 1887, incorporated Hekate into their magical system as an important goddess associated with crossroads, magic and the deeper mysteries (Regardie, 1989). Their rituals and teachings, while not centred on Hekate specifically, acknowledged her as a powerful triple goddess with dominion over earth, sea and sky. Concurrently, academic studies of ancient Greek religion began to recognise Hekate's complex historical role. The pioneering work of scholars like Jane Ellen Harrison in *Prolegomena to the Study of Greek Religion* (1903) highlighted Hekate's pre-Olympian origins and her evolution from a powerful goddess of many spheres to her later, more limited association with witchcraft and the underworld.

Early 20th Century: Occult Renaissance
The early 20th century marked Hekate's incorporation into modern occult systems, most notably in the works of Aleister Crowley and the development of the Wiccan religion. Crowley, who founded Thelema, referenced Hekate in various writings, associating her with lunar magic and the darker aspects of feminine power (Crowley, 1929). Though not central to his system, she represented certain magical currents within his complex cosmology. More significantly, Gerald Gardner's formulation of Wicca in the 1940s and 1950s drew upon the concept of the triple goddess, with Hekate often

associated with the crone aspect of the maiden – mother – crone triad (Gardner, 1954). This interpretation, whilst somewhat reductive compared to her ancient roles, nevertheless secured Hekate a place in modern pagan practice.

Doreen Valiente, who collaborated with Gardner and wrote much of the early Wiccan liturgical material, included invocations that referenced Hekate's powers, particularly her association with crossroads and transitions (Valiente, 1962). These elements became embedded in Wiccan ritual structure, ensuring Hekate's continued relevance in modern paganism. The scholarly understanding of Hekate also evolved during this period.

Works such as Theodor Krause's *Hekatestudien* (1914) provided more nuanced analyses of her historical worship and theological significance, laying groundwork for later academic and spiritual explorations of her cult.

Late 20th Century: Neopagan Resurgence
The final decades of the 20th century witnessed an unprecedented growth in interest in Hekate among neopagan and reconstructionist movements. This period saw a shift from viewing Hekate primarily through the lens of Wiccan theology to more historically informed

approaches that sought to understand and revive her ancient worship. Publications such as *The Rotting Goddess* by Jacob Rabinowitz (1998) explored her darker associations, while other practitioners emphasised her roles as a guide, midwife of souls, and keeper of wisdom.

From the 1970s, the feminist spirituality movement, exemplified by works like *The Spiral Dance* by Starhawk (1979), embraced Hekate as an embodiment of feminine power and wisdom that had been suppressed by patriarchal religions. This interpretation fuelled interest in reclaiming Hekate as a central goddess in many forms of magical and theurgic practice. Sarah Iles Johnston's *Hekate Soteira* (1990) provided a comprehensive academic study of Hekate's role in Greek religion that influenced both scholarly understanding and magical practice. This more history-centric approach has led to the establishment of groups specifically dedicated to Hekate's worship, such as the Covenant of Hekate, which formed in the early 21st century.

Her veneration spanned diverse traditions, from eclectic Wiccan covens to strict reconstructionist groups such as Hellenismos, which reconstructs ancient Greek religious practices, Nova Roma, which reconstructs the Roman religion, the Hermetic Order of the

Golden Dawn and the Hermetic Brotherhood of Luxor, which draw from historical occult traditions. The late 20th century also saw the beginning of academic conferences dedicated to studying Hekate, bringing together scholars and practitioners in unprecedented dialogue. This cross-fertilisation between academic study and spiritual practice characterised the modern revival of interest in Hekate and set the stage for her continued significance in contemporary paganism.

In this first chapter, I wanted to illustrate how complex Hekate is. Whatever origin you choose to accept, it is apparent that for millennia Hekate has been an accompanying powerful goddess whose power and magic is so enduring that even today she thrives, presenting herself in whatever way she chooses.

Each person that walks with Hekate finds her in their own way, or maybe more accurately, in the way she determines. Most people that I have talked to that follow Hekate or Hekatean magickal practices have told me that they did not choose Hekate, but rather they felt they were tasked to do something. Sometimes they resisted for a while but finally knew the path they had to take.

HEKATE AND HER SISTERS

'I am she that is the natural mother of all things, mistress and governess of all the elements, the initial progeny of worlds, chief of powers divine, Queen of Heaven, the principal of the Gods celestial, the light of the goddesses: at my will the planets of the air, the wholesome winds of the seas, and the silences of Hell be disposed; my name, my divinity is adored throughout all the world in divers manners, in variable customs and in many names, for the Phrygians call me the mother of the Gods: the Athenians, Minerva: the Cyprians, Venus: the Candians, Diana: the Sicilians Proserpina: the Eleusians, Ceres: some Juno, other Bellona, other Hecate: and principally the Ethiopians which dwell in the Orient, and the Egyptians which are excellent in all kind of ancient doctrine, and by their proper ceremonies accustom to worship mee, do call me Queen Isis.' Lucius Apuleius - The Golden Ass, Book II Chapter 47

The One, Three and Many Faces of Hekate
An initial dive into understanding Hekate, her roots and attributes can seem a demanding task. There is already a large and growing corpus of work that often feels contradictory. There are many names or epithets given to Hekate, each reflecting a different aspect of her role or energy.

To make this even more confusing, some of these epithets are also used to honour other goddesses. There are also examples of when one goddess appears to have morphed into another.

To help think about these overlaps, there are three ways to ways to look at this; the first is syncretism, which is the amalgamation religions, cultures, or schools of thought. For example, in Plutarch's *On Isis and Osiris* (1st–2nd century CE), he notes that 'some call Isis by the name of Athena, others Hekate'. This text suggests that educated Greeks conceptually linked these goddesses despite their distinct cultural origins. Syncretism is commonly found in the Roman approach to existing religious and cultural practices where, for example, Hekate is transformed into Trivia––the triple faced Roman goddess. A second way of thinking about the blurring of goddess boundaries is the Aspect Theory, where Enodia may have been understood as a specific aspect or description of Hekate. Finally, there is also a consideration of regional variation, such as when a local goddess shared attributes with Hekate which led to frequent associations but not necessarily a complete merging of identities. For example, it has been argued that the goddess Enodia, who was primarily worshipped in ancient Thessaly and was well known in Hellenistic Macedonia.

Enodia is a goddess of roads, protection, ghosts, purification, the city, and cemeteries. Enodia appears to have gradually been absorbed into the more widely worshipped Hekate, particularly as Greek religious practices became more standardised. Finally, I have always liked the concept which derives from Procrustes who, was a robber living in Attica. Procrustes had an iron bed on which he compelled his victims to lie. If a victim was shorter than the bed, Procrustes stretched them. Alternatively, if the victim was longer than the bed, he cut off the legs to make the body fit the bed's length. In either event the victim always died. Today we still honour Procrustes, not by taking human victims, but taking ideas and concepts and either stretching them or cutting them to make them fit our view of the world and save us the trouble of having to do more research or think harder about something. I suspect there is quite a lot of procrustean work happens with Hekate today, with people not being prepared to do enough research, or too ready to accept all they are told and jump to conclusions without looking at all the evidence available. With the proliferation of badly produced AI books, with 'authors' that have not bothered to verify and triangulate their sources and research; shoddy work becomes a part of the new corpus of work on Hekate, regardless of its accuracy.

What's in a Name?

The many names or epithets with which Hekate is honoured is another source of confusion. Here are some of the most common, with archaeological and literary examples.

Soteira (Saviour) [Σώτειρα], Soteira emerges from Ptolemaic Egyptian contexts, representing Hekate's profound protective capabilities. More than a simple protective deity, Soteira embodies the concept of spiritual preservation and healing. In magical and religious practices, this name invoked Hekate's power to rescue individuals from physical dangers and metaphysical threats, suggesting a guardian role that transcended traditional divine boundaries.

The earliest archaeological evidence for Hekate Soteira comes from inscriptions found in Asia Minor dating to the 3rd century BCE, particularly in ancient Caria and Ionia. A notable example is a marble altar discovered at Stratonikeia, bearing a dedication to Hekate Soteira Epiphanestata (most manifest saviour Hekate), dating to approximately 200 BCE.

In literary sources, the title appears prominently in the *Chaldean Oracles*, which present Hekate as a powerful cosmic force responsible for mediating between gods and humanity.

The *Chaldean Oracles* portray Hekate Soteira as 'the saviour not merely of bodies but of souls,' suggesting her role extended beyond physical protection to spiritual salvation. Plutarch (1st–2nd century CE) mentions Hekate Soteira in his *Moralia*, connecting her salvation aspects to her role in guiding souls at life's transitions. He describes rituals performed at crossroads where Hekate was invoked as Soteira to protect travellers and those undergoing significant life changes.

Phosphoros, (Light-Bringer) [Φωσφόρος], which will undoubtedly prick up the ears of all Luciferians reading this. This name is found in the *Homeric Hymn to Demeter*, and Phosphoros represents Hekate's most iconic spiritual function. It symbolises her ability to illuminate not merely physical darkness, but spiritual obscurity. Her torches became metaphorical representations of knowledge, revealing hidden truths and guiding souls through transformative experiences. The light she brings is understood as epistemological revelation — an illumination of understanding beyond mere visual perception.

The earliest literary evidence of Hekate as Phosphoros appears in the *Homeric Hymn to Demeter*, where Hekate is described as coming to meet Persephone and Demeter with a light:

'Hecate, with a torch in her hands, met them' (line 52). While the exact title Phosphoros is not used in the hymn itself, this representation established the iconographic tradition of Hekate as torchbearer that would later be associated with the Phosphoros epithet (Rayor, 2014). Archaeological evidence for Hekate Phosphoros includes numerous votive reliefs and statues from the 5th–4th centuries BCE depicting the goddess holding torches. A particularly significant example is a marble relief from Aegina (circa 430 BCE, now in the Berlin State Museums) showing Hekate with torches accompanying Persephone's return from the underworld. The name appears explicitly in Aristophanes' *Frogs* (405 BCE), where Hekate is invoked as Phosphoros Hekate during a journey to the underworld, highlighting her role as guide between worlds. Later, Euripides refers to her as the 'torch-bearing Hekate' in *Helen* (412 BCE), further cementing this association. Apollonius of Rhodes in the *Argonautica* (3rd century BCE) refers to her as a 'daughter of Perses' who illuminates the night, creating a connection between Hekate and cosmic light. While Phosphoros later became associated with Lucifer in Christian contexts, its original Greek usage was applied to several deities associated with light, including Artemis and Eos, and referred simply to the function of bringing illumination.

Kleidouchos [Κλειδοῦχος)] meaning key-holder or key-bearer, represents Hekate's function as a gatekeeper between different realms and states of being. This title emphasises her ability to unlock passages and grant access to hidden knowledge or closed domains. The earliest archaeological evidence for Hekate as key-bearer comes from votive reliefs dating to the 5th–4th centuries BCE. A significant example is a marble relief from Thasos (circa 375–350 BCE) depicting Hekate holding keys alongside other attributes such as torches and serpents. Keys appear as one of her attributes on coins from various Greek cities, particularly in Asia Minor, dating from the 4th century BCE onwards. In literature, the association between Hekate and keys emerges most prominently in the Orphic tradition. The *Orphic Hymn to Hekate* (composed between the 3rd century BCE and the 2nd century CE) directly addresses her as 'key-bearing queen of the entire cosmos' (κλειδοῦχ', κόσμου κλειδοῦχε μέδουσα), establishing her cosmic significance as controller of access between worlds. Theocritus, in his second *Idyll* (3rd century BCE), portrays a woman performing magical rituals who invokes Hekate's power over 'the adamantine gates of Hades', implicitly referencing her key-holding function. This text provides evidence for how Hekate's Kleidouchos aspect was understood in popular magical practice.

Pausanias, in his *Description of Greece* (2nd century CE), describes a sanctuary at Eleusis containing a statue of Hekate Propylaia (Before the Gates), which scholars have connected to her Kleidouchos aspect. This archaeological reference suggests that by the Roman period, Hekate's role as gatekeeper had become established in cult practice. This title gained particular significance in late antiquity, especially in Neoplatonic philosophy. Proclus (5th century CE) elaborates on Hekate's role as Kleidouchos in his commentary on Plato's *Timaeus*, describing her as the deity who controls access to different levels of reality.

Trioditis [Τριοδῖτις], meaning 'of the three ways' or 'of the crossroads', represents one of Hekate's most fundamental aspects, emphasising her dominion over places where paths intersect. This title underscores her role as guardian of liminal spaces and moments of decision. The earliest literary evidence for Hekate's association with crossroads appears in Sophocles' fragmentary play, *Root Cutters* (5th century BCE), though the specific epithet Trioditis is not explicitly used. Aristophanes provides more direct evidence in his comedy *Plutus* (388 BCE), where characters discuss leaving offerings to Hekate at the triodoi (crossroads), implying her established cult connection to these locations.

The title Trioditis itself appears explicitly in Theocritus' *Idyll 2* (3rd century BCE), where the character Simaetha calls upon Hekate Trioditis during a love spell ritual performed at a crossroads. This text substantiates both the epithet's use and its ritual context. Archaeological evidence for Hekate Trioditis includes numerous small triple-formed statues (Hekataia) found at ancient crossroads throughout Greece, dating from the 5th century BCE onwards. Particularly significant examples include a marble Hekataion discovered at the intersection of three roads in the Athenian Agora (circa 430-420 BCE). This three-bodied representation visually reinforces her association with triple crossroads. Inscriptional evidence from Athens documents the practice of setting up Hekataia at crossroads, including a 5th century BCE decree describing the installation of a statue of Hekate Trioditis at a prominent intersection.

Additionally, archaeological excavations at crossroads throughout the Greek world have uncovered the remains of small shrines and votive deposits dedicated to Hekate, including clay figurines, lamps and ritual vessels. The 2nd century CE geographer Pausanias, in his *Description of Greece*, mentions a triple-formed statue of Hekate at a crossroads in Aegina, attributed to the sculptor Myron, further attesting to the longevity of this association.

Later magical papyri from Graeco-Roman Egypt (3rd–4th centuries CE) contain numerous spells invoking Hekate Trioditis, confirming the epithet's continued ritual significance.

Chthonia (Χθονία), means 'of the earth' or 'of the underworld,' connects Hekate to subterranean realms and chthonic powers. This title emphasises her role in mediating between the world of the living and the realm of the dead. The conceptual foundation for Hekate's chthonic aspect appears in Hesiod's *Theogony* (c. 700 BCE), which grants her 'privilege both in earth, and in heaven, and in sea' (lines 413–414), establishing her triple domain that includes the underworld. While the specific epithet Chthonia is not used in this text, Hesiod's description provides the mythological basis for her later chthonic associations (Most, 2006). The earliest direct literary attestation of Hekate as Chthonia comes from Aeschylus' fragmentary play *Psychagogoi* (Soul-Raisers, early 5th century BCE), where the designation appears in an invocation to chthonic deities. This suggests that by the early Classical period, the epithet was already established in religious practice. Archaeological evidence for Hekate's chthonic aspect includes votive reliefs depicting her with underworld attributes, such as a 4th century BCE marble relief from Eleusis showing Hekate with torches alongside other chthonic deities.

The discovery of Hekate figurines in burial contexts, particularly in Southern Italy and Sicily from the 4th–3rd centuries BCE, further attests to her chthonic associations. There are inscriptions on a 3rd century BCE altar from Rhodes dedicated to Hekate Chthonia, explicitly documenting the epithet's use in cult practice. Additionally, lead curse tablets (defixiones) from the 4th century BCE onwards frequently invoke Hekate alongside other chthonic deities, reflecting her perceived power over the underworld.

In later literature, Apollodorus' *Library* (1st–2nd century CE) explicitly identifies Hekate as a chthonic goddess, while magical papyri from Graeco-Roman Egypt contain numerous spells invoking Hekate Chthonia for necromantic purposes. The 5th century CE Neoplatonist philosopher Proclus, in his commentary on Plato's Cratylus, elaborates on Hekate's chthonic nature, interpreting it in terms of metaphysical principles relating to manifestation and material existence.

Antaia (Ἀνταία), meaning 'who meets' or 'who encounters', emphasises Hekate's quality of sudden appearance and direct intervention in human affairs. This title suggests her capacity for immediate presence and unexpected manifestation, particularly at critical moments.

It also suggests the practice of divine encounter (theophaneia), where ritual specialists undertake direct communication with deities. This interpretation aligns with archaeological evidence for incubation practices at some of Hekate's sanctuaries, particularly in Asia Minor, where worshippers sought direct encounters with the goddess through dream or vision.

The earliest evidence for this name appears in fragmentary lyric poetry attributed to Bacchylides (5th century BCE), where Hekate Antaia is invoked in what appears to be a context of supplication or prayer. However, due to the fragmentary nature of this text, the full context remains unclear. More substantial literary evidence comes from Apollonius Rhodius' *Argonautica* (3rd century BCE), where the epithet is used in a passage describing Medea's magical preparations. The text connects Hekate Antaia with nocturnal appearances and magical knowledge, suggesting her role as a deity who manifests directly to practitioners of magic. Archaeological evidence for Hekate Antaia is less explicit than for her other designations, but there are votive reliefs showing Hekate emerging from the earth or appearing suddenly to worshippers, such as examples from 4th century BCE Athens and Asia Minor.

Epigraphic evidence includes a 2nd century CE inscription from Lagina, where Hekate's major sanctuary was located, referencing rituals related to her quality of sudden manifestation. While the specific epithet Antaia is not preserved in this inscription, the described practices align with the concept of encountering the goddess. This epithet gains prominence in magical texts from the Hellenistic and Roman periods. The Greek Magical Papyri (PGM IV.2708-84, circa 3rd–4th century CE) contain invocations to Hekate Antaia in spells designed to summon the goddess for direct consultation, highlighting the epithet's association with divine epiphany and manifestation.

Enodia (Ἐνοδία) [Of the roadways] etymologically derives from the Greek 'en' (in) and ὁδός (road), literally meaning 'she who is in the road' or 'of the roadways'. This epithet emphasises Hekate's role as a guardian of travellers and crossroads. The concept of Enodia transcended mere physical protection, symbolising guidance through life's metaphorical journeys.

In the *Orphic Hymn to Hekate* (3rd–2nd century BCE), she is invoked as Enodia who 'brings light to the obscure road of life', suggesting her role in spiritual navigation and transitions between life stages.

The earliest literary references to linking Enodia to Hekate appear in Pindar's works, particularly in fragments of his poetry dating to the 5th century BCE. In his *Paean to Hekate*, Pindar portrays her as a protective deity who guides travellers safely along their journeys. Pindar's representation highlights how Enodia was invoked for protection during physical travels in the ancient world. Archaeological evidence for the worship of Hekate as Enodia comes prominently from Thessaly, where inscriptions dating from the 5th–4th centuries BCE have been discovered. The Archaeological Museum of Larissa houses several votive offerings and boundary markers (horoi) inscribed with dedications to Enodia, revealing a particularly strong cult presence in northern Greece. A notable archaeological find includes a 4th century BCE marble relief from Pherae showing Enodia with torches, emphasising her role as a light-bringer on dark paths.

Propylaia (Προπυλαία) [Of the Gate] derives from 'pro' (before) and 'pylē' (gate), designating Hekate as the guardian who stands before gates and entrances. This title emphasises her liminal nature as a goddess of thresholds and boundaries. The earliest textual references to Hekate as Propylaia appear in Aeschylus' works, particularly in fragments of his lost plays from the early 5th century BCE.

Archaeological evidence is more abundant, with dedications to Hekate Propylaia found at the entrance to the Acropolis in Athens, dating to approximately 430–420 BCE. These small shrines, known as Hekataia, were deliberately positioned at the monumental gateway (also called the Propylaia) of the Acropolis, establishing a literal and symbolic connection between the goddess and this architectural threshold. Excavations at Eleusis yield further evidence of Hekate's association with this title.

A 4th century BCE inscription discovered at the sanctuary entrance mentions offerings to Propylaia, and a small temple dedicated to Hekate stood near the main gate of the Eleusinian sanctuary. This positioning reinforced her role as guardian of the mystical threshold between the mundane world and the sacred realm of the Eleusinian Mysteries. The symbolic significance of Propylaia extends beyond physical gates. In the *Chaldean Oracles* (2nd century CE), Hekate is described as the 'Propylaia of all divine mysteries,' suggesting her role as gatekeeper between different states of consciousness and spiritual understanding. This metaphysical interpretation of the epithet reveals how Hekate's gate-keeping functions evolved from physical protection to spiritual guidance through transformative passages.

Brimo (Βριμώ) (The Mighty One) derives from the Greek verb 'brimaomai,' meaning 'to rage' or 'to terrify,' emphasising the fearsome and powerful aspects of Hekate's nature. This description suggests a raw, primordial divine power. The earliest substantial literary reference to Hekate as Brimo appears in Apollonius Rhodius' *Argonautica* (3rd century BCE). In Book 3, Medea prepares to invoke 'Brimo, the night-wanderer' in a midnight ritual. The text presents Brimo as a terrifying chthonic goddess associated with night, magic, and necromancy.

Archaeological evidence for the specific worship of Hekate as Brimo is more limited than for her other epithets. However, excavations at the Temple of Artemis at Brauron revealed several 4th century BCE votive tablets with dedications to a deity called Brimo, which has been connected to Hekate. Additionally, lead curse tablets (defixiones) from various Greek sites dating from the 4th–2nd centuries BCE occasionally invoke Brimo alongside other chthonic deities when calling for powerful magical intervention.

The *Orphic Argonautica* (4th–6th century CE) expands upon earlier literary references, describing elaborate rituals to Brimo involving night-time invocations and animal sacrifices.

This text portrays Brimo as a goddess of tremendous magical potential who must be approached with the utmost respect and caution. This title also appears in connection with the Eleusinian Mysteries. Clement of Alexandria's *Protrepticus* (2nd century CE) mentions that in the secret rites, Brimo was invoked as part of the most sacred ceremonies, suggesting this aspect of Hekate was particularly associated with mystical transformation and the raw power needed to facilitate spiritual rebirth.

Propolos (Πρόπολος), meaning 'attendant,' 'guide,' or 'escort', highlights Hekate's role as a spiritual companion who leads individuals through transitions and liminal experiences. This name emphasises her function as a protective guardian who accompanies souls on difficult journeys. The earliest significant literary attestation of Hekate as Propolos appears in Euripides' *Ion* (c. 414–412 BCE). Although not using the exact title, Euripides portrays Hekate as the attendant (προπόλευμα) of Persephone, establishing her role as a divine guide associated with underworld journeys. This connection is developed further in the *Homeric Hymn to Demeter* (7th–6th centuries BCE), where Hekate acts as a guide and companion to both Persephone and Demeter, though again without the specific epithet being used.

The name Propolos also appears in Aeschylus' fragmentary plays, particularly in references preserved by later authors. The Byzantine encyclopaedia *Suda* (10th century CE) cites Aeschylus as using this designation for Hekate, suggesting its presence in works now lost. Archaeological evidence supporting Hekate's guiding aspect includes votive reliefs from the 5th–4th centuries BCE depicting her leading Persephone from the underworld, such as examples found at Eleusis. These visual representations, while not explicitly labelled with the name, reinforce her role as divine escort. Inscriptional evidence for the epithet includes dedicatory texts from Asia Minor dating to the 3rd–2nd centuries BCE, where Hekate is honoured as Propolos in contexts suggesting her role as guide through spiritual or physical journeys. This honour appears in frequent inscriptions from Lagina. Apollonius Rhodius' *Argonautica* (3rd century BCE) develops Hekate's guiding aspect, describing her as an escort through magical workings and supernatural encounters. While not using the specific epithet Propolos, this text elaborates on the concept of Hekate as mystical guide. The Neoplatonic philosopher Proclus (5th century CE) provides philosophical interpretation of Hekate as Propolos in his commentary on Plato's *Timaeus*, describing her as the guide who leads souls through cosmic transitions and metaphysical boundaries.

This later philosophical development demonstrates the epithet's evolution from literal guide to metaphysical concept.

Dadouchos (Δαδοῦχος), meaning 'torchbearer,' emphasises Hekate's role as a deity who brings illumination and revelation. This title connects her to sacred mysteries and initiation rituals, particularly those involving transformative spiritual experiences. The earliest literary associations between Hekate and torches appear in the *Homeric Hymn to Demeter* (7th–6th centuries BCE), which describes her meeting Persephone while holding splendid torches (lines 52–53). While the specific title Dadouchos is not used in this early text, it establishes the iconographic tradition that would later be associated with this title. The name gains particular significance in the context of the Eleusinian Mysteries, where the Dadouchos was one of the principal priests who held torches during the sacred procession and ritual. Archaeological evidence from Eleusis includes inscriptions dating from the 4th century BCE onwards that mention the office of Dadouchos in connection with Hekate's cult. A particularly significant inscription from Eleusis records a dedication by a priest who served as a Dadouchos, mentioning Hekate alongside Demeter and Kore (Persephone), suggesting her integral role in the mysteries and her association with this torch-bearing function.

Artistic representations of Hekate as torchbearer are abundant in ancient Greek art from the 5th century BCE onwards. Notable examples include a red-figure on a lekythos which is a single handled terracotta flask, from c. 460–450 BCE showing Hekate with torches in the context of Persephone's story, and numerous votive reliefs depicting her with twin torches. Literary evidence from the Hellenistic period includes Theocritus' *Idyll 2* (3rd century BCE), which describes Hekate with shining torches in the context of magical rituals, suggesting that by this period her torch-bearing aspect had become central to her identity in popular religion.

Later magical texts, particularly the Greek Magical Papyri (PGM IV.2785–2890, 3rd–4th centuries CE), contain invocations to Hekate Dadouchos, highlighting her role in illuminating magical workings and revelatory experiences. These texts connect her torch-bearing function explicitly with her ability to bring spiritual illumination and revelation. The 2nd century CE writer Pausanias, in his *Description of Greece* (1.38.6), mentions a statue of Hekate holding torches at the entrance to the Eleusinian sanctuary, confirming the visual representation of this aspect of the goddess in cult contexts.

Krataiis (Κραταιίς), meaning 'the strong one' or 'the powerful,' emphasises Hekate's supernatural might and authority and her formidable nature and capacity for effective intervention in human affairs. The earliest known literary reference of Krataiis appears in Homer's *Odyssey* (c. 8th century BCE), where it is used as the name of the mother of the monster Scylla. This reference does not explicitly identify Krataiis with Hekate. However, the identification of Hekate with Krataiis appears in Apollonius Rhodius' *Argonautica* (3rd century BCE), where Medea invokes Hekate Krataiis during magical operations. This text provides examples for the use in magical contexts and its association with Hekate's capacity for supernatural interventions.

The distinction features prominently in the Orphic tradition, appearing in the *Orphic Hymn to Hekate* (composed between the 3rd–2nd centuries BCE), where she is addressed as 'Krataiis' in the context of her cosmic power and authority over various domains. Archaeological evidence for the use of this name includes a lead curse tablet (defixio) from 4th century BCE Athens invoking Hekate Krataiis to enforce a binding spell, suggesting a connection to magical practices seeking to harness divine power.

There is also inscriptional evidence including a 2nd century CE altar from Asia Minor dedicated to Hekate Krataiis, which suggests a transition from primarily magical contexts to more formal religious worship. This title gained particular prominence in magical texts from the Hellenistic and Roman periods. The Greek Magical Papyri contain numerous spells invoking Hekate Krataiis, emphasising her tremendous power in magical operations. These texts often pair this title with elaborate praise of Hekate's cosmic authority and supernatural might. Neoplatonic philosophers including Porphyry and Proclus (3rd–5th centuries CE) interpreted Hekate Krataiis in metaphysical terms, seeing her as representing the powerful demiurgic forces that shape the material cosmos. This philosophical reinterpretation demonstrates the epithet's evolution from a simple descriptor of divine strength to a complex, cosmological principle.

Angelos (Ἄγγελος), meaning 'messenger', highlights Hekate's role as an intermediary between different cosmic realms. This name emphasises her function as a divine messenger who traverses boundaries between the mortal world, the underworld, and the celestial sphere. The earliest identifiable association of Hekate with the Angelos designation appears in fragmentary references from Sophocles' lost play, *The Root-Cutters* (5th century BCE), where she is described as a messenger between worlds. However, the connection becomes more explicit in later sources. The 5th century CE Neoplatonist Proclus, in his *Commentary on Plato's Timaeus*, elaborates on Hekate as Angelos. He describes her as the crucial intermediary force who connects the intelligible and sensible realms, serving as a cosmic messenger who facilitates communication between different levels of reality. Proclus writes that:

'Hekate as Angelos stands at the crossroads of divine realms, transmitting the ineffable wisdom of the higher gods to those below.'

This reflects some of the core aspects of the Cosmic World Soul conception from the *Chaldean Oracles*. Archaeological evidence for the worship of Hekate as Angelos is less abundant than literary references. However, inscriptions from 3rd–4th century CE, found in temples in Asia Minor, particularly from sites near Lagina, include dedications to Hekate Angelos. A notable archaeological find includes a 3rd century CE marble altar from Ephesus with relief carvings depicting Hekate in triple form alongside the inscription ΑΓΓΕΛΟΣ, suggesting her messenger aspect was venerated in this region.

The concept of Angelos gained particular significance in the syncretistic religious environment of Hellenistic and Roman Egypt. The Greek Magical Papyri contains several spells invoking Hekate Angelos as a powerful intermediary who could carry petitions to other deities and bring back divine responses. In these texts, she is often portrayed as uniquely capable of traversing cosmic boundaries, described as 'she who moves freely between the worlds of light and darkness'.

Nykteria (Νυκτερία), meaning 'of the night' or 'nocturnal one,' emphasises Hekate's profound connection to darkness, night-time, and the mysteries that unfold under the cover of darkness. This name reinforces her association with liminal times and spaces, particularly the threshold between day and night. The earliest explicit literary references to Hekate as Nykteria appear in PGM IV, known as *The Spell of Attraction*, Hekate is invoked as Nykteria, 'goddess of the crossroads, who commands the night'. This text portrays her as the quintessential nocturnal deity who holds dominion over the hours of darkness, and the magical operations conducted during this time. Archaeological evidence for the worship of Hekate as Nykteria includes several votive offerings found in cave sanctuaries across Greece and Asia Minor.

A particularly significant find comes from the Cave of the Nymphs at Vari (Attica), where a 2nd century CE inscription dedicates a small shrine to 'Hekate Nykteria, guardian of the night hours'. This underground sanctuary, with its perpetual darkness, served as an appropriate setting for the worship of Hekate in her nocturnal aspect. The concept of Nykteria gained additional prominence in the *Chaldean Oracles* where Hekate is described as 'Nykteria, she who illuminates the primordial darkness', suggesting her role not merely as a goddess of night but as one who brings understanding and illumination to the darkness of ignorance and chaos. The Archaeological Museum of Thessaloniki houses a 3rd century CE black basalt statue of Hekate with the inscription NYKTEPIA, showing the goddess in triple form with six raised torches. In the *Orphic Hymn to Hekate* (3rd–2nd century BCE), she is described as 'torch-bearing Nykteria' who 'rejoices in the darkness' yet paradoxically brings clarity and vision. This portrayal highlights the paradoxical nature of Hekate Nykteria — a deity who embodies darkness but simultaneously offers illumination and understanding within that darkness. The Roman author Apuleius, in *The Golden Ass* (2nd century CE), refers to Hekate's nocturnal aspect when describing mystical initiations that take place at night under her protection.

While not using the exact epithet Nykteria, his description of 'Hekate, goddess of the threefold night' clearly aligns with this aspect of her worship.

Einalia (Εἰναλία), meaning 'of the sea' or 'she who dwells in the sea', is a less commonly discussed aspect of Hekate's multifaceted nature. This name highlights her connection to marine environments and her authority extending beyond her more frequently recognised terrestrial and chthonic domains. The earliest literary associations between Hekate and marine aspects appear in oblique references from Hesiod's *Theogony* (c. 700 BCE), where she is granted dominion over earth, sea, and sky by Zeus. However, the specific title Einalia emerges more explicitly in later texts. An early mention comes from a fragmentary hymn attributed to Alcaeus (c. 6th century BCE), which invokes 'Einalia, guardian of sailors and harbours'. There is archaeological evidence for Hekate's worship as Einalia is particularly concentrated in coastal communities throughout the ancient Mediterranean. Notable finds include a 4th century BCE marble stele discovered near Piraeus (Athens' port) bearing the inscription 'To Hekate Einalia, Protector of Mariners'. This votive offering, likely dedicated by sailors or merchants, established a direct connection between Hekate and maritime protection.

The temple complex at Lagina has several inscriptions dating from the 2nd century BCE–2nd century CE that reference Einalia among Hekate's titles.

Archaeological examination of the temple's frieze reveals subtle marine iconography such as waves, sea creatures and nautical elements interspersed among more traditional representations of the goddess, suggesting her maritime associations were incorporated into formal worship. Excavations at coastal shrines in Cyprus and Rhodes have uncovered small bronze anchors and ship models dedicated to Hekate Einalia, dating to the Hellenistic period (3rd–1st centuries BCE). These offerings, likely made by seafarers seeking divine protection, demonstrate the practical application of Hekate's marine aspect in the lives of those who navigated the Mediterranean Sea.

The 2nd century CE geographer Pausanias, in his *Description of Greece,* mentions a coastal shrine to 'Hekate of the Sea' near Hermione in the Peloponnese, where annual night-time rituals were conducted to ensure safe passage for local fishing fleets. While not using the exact term Einalia, his description clearly aligns with this aspect of her worship. The PGM also contain several spells invoking Hekate Einalia in rituals connected to sea voyages, fishing expeditions, and weather manipulation including invocations to 'Einalia, mistress of the tidal depths' alongside instructions for creating a protective amulet for sea travel. In philosophical writings, particularly those of the Neoplatonists, Hekate Einalia acquired symbolic dimensions beyond literal maritime associations. Porphyry's *On Images* (3rd century CE) interprets Hekate's connection to the sea as representing 'the fluid nature of creation and dissolution,' portraying Einalia as a representation of cosmic processes reflected in the sea's constant movement and transformation.

The symbolism of Einalia extends beyond mere geographical dominion over oceans. The seas with its mysterious depths, changing tides and liminal position between known and unknown worlds serves as a metaphor for Hekate's nature as the goddess of boundaries and transitions. Just as the shoreline represents the threshold between land and sea, Hekate Einalia stands at the boundary between different states of being.

The maritime aspect of Hekate also connects her to the broader tradition of Mediterranean Sea goddesses, including Amphitrite and aspects of Artemis and Aphrodite, demonstrating the complex syncretism characteristic of Greco-Roman religious practice.

However, what distinguishes Hekate Einalia is her simultaneous connection to both terrestrial crossroads and marine pathways, positioning her as guardian of all journeys, whether by land or sea. However, there are several connections between Hekate and other important goddesses, and in the next section I will explore some of the key relationships.

The Divine Connections of Hekate: Syncretism and Associations

The Carian Hekate has strong associations with civic authority and protection, as evidenced by the prominence of her sanctuary and its role in local governance. There are possible connections to earlier Anatolian mother goddess traditions, suggested by certain iconographic elements and ritual practices. The sanctuary of Hekate at Lagina provides significant archaeological evidence for her Carian worship.

The temple complex, dating to the Hellenistic period is built upon earlier foundations, that suggests a long-standing cultic tradition. Votive offerings found at the site evidence continuous worship from at least the 6th century BCE throughout the Roman period. These artefacts suggest evolution in how Hekate was perceived and worshipped over time. The temple frieze, dated to approximately 125 BCE, depicts scenes related to Hekate's veneration.

The evidence suggests a goddess who held both civic and cosmic significance. Inscriptions from Lagina include sacred laws and festival regulations that illuminate the nature of Hekate's worship. These inscriptions are primarily in Greek but also contain Carian features. Strabo's *Geography* mentions the importance of Hekate's sanctuary at Lagina, describing it as a major religious centre. His account, while dating to the late 1st century BCE, suggests knowledge of older traditions. The Byzantine lexicographer Stephanus of Byzantium preserves fragments of earlier sources regarding Carian religious practices, including references to Hekate's worship. Both the Carian and Greek manifestations of Hecate share certain foundational characteristics:

1. **Torch-bearing**: Throughout her various manifestations, Hecate is consistently associated with torches, which become symbols of illumination in darkness.

2. **Liminal Associations**: While more pronounced in her Greek form, both manifestations of Hecate have some connection to boundaries and thresholds, though the emphasis differs significantly.

3. **Protective Functions**: In both contexts, Hecate serves protective functions, though in Caria this appears as broader civic protection rather than the more specialised protection at doorways and crossroads emphasised in Greek contexts.

The differences between the Carian and Greek Hekate reveal much about the process of religious transmission and transformation. The Carian Hecate was a major, central deity with broad domains. In terms of the chthonic aspects, the Greek Hekate developed pronounced associations with the underworld, ghosts, and the dead that appear less prominent in Carian contexts.

In Caria, particularly at Lagina, Hekate's worship was integrated into public civic religion and even political structures, with her priesthood holding significant civic authority. In Greek contexts, while not exclusive to private worship, Hekate's rituals often took place at liminal locations like crossroads and in private homes, somewhat removed from central civic cult. The triple form so emblematic of Greek and Roman Hecate are largely absent from Carian representations, suggesting a significant conceptual shift in how the goddess was understood.

Hekate and Artemis

The connection between Hekate and Artemis represents one of the most enduring divine associations in Greek religion. Both goddesses shared dominion over liminal spaces, with Artemis ruling the wilderness and Hekate governing crossroads and thresholds. The earliest literary evidence linking these goddesses appears in the *Homeric Hymn to Demeter* (c. 7th–6th century BCE), where Artemis witnesses Persephone's abduction and Hekate reports to Demeter having heard Persephone's cries. While maintaining distinct identities in this narrative, their cooperative actions establish an early conceptual connection.

Archaeological evidence for their association emerges prominently in 5th–4th century BCE Athens, where votive reliefs occasionally depicted Hekate with Artemis's bow and hunting dogs. The Archaeological Museum of Athens houses several examples of these syncretistic representations, including a notable 4th century BCE marble relief showing a triple-formed Hekate with attributes typically associated with Artemis.

The shared designation Phosphoros (Light-Bringer) appears in inscriptions for both goddesses. A 3rd century BCE inscription from Delos invokes Artemis-Hekate Phosphoros, suggesting a formal cultic recognition of their overlapping identities. Similarly, a 2nd century BCE dedication from the Temple of Artemis in Ephesus addresses 'Artemis of the Crossroads', adopting terminology typically associated with Hekate. Pausanias (2nd century CE) documents this connection in his *Description of Greece*, noting a sanctuary at Aegina where 'the same priestess serves both Hekate and Artemis'. This reference suggests that their worship occasionally merged in practical cult activities, with shared priesthoods and sacred spaces.

Hekate and Persephone
The relationship between Hekate and Persephone stems primarily from their shared chthonic associations and roles in the Eleusinian Mysteries. Their connection first appears prominently in the *Homeric Hymn to Demeter*, where Hekate becomes Persephone's companion after her return from the underworld. Archaeological evidence from Eleusis supports this literary association. Excavations have revealed several 5th–4th century BCE votive reliefs depicting Hekate alongside Persephone and Demeter, often in scenes representing the central myth of the Mysteries. These artefacts confirm Hekate's integration into the core Eleusinian narrative and ritual structure.

Chthonia (Of the Earth/Underworld) was applied to both goddesses, as evidenced by inscriptions from various Greek sites. A notable 3rd century BCE inscription from Selinunte, Sicily, references a dedication to Persephone and Hekate Chthonia, demonstrating their shared dominion over underworld realms. In magical contexts, in the PGM, Hekate and Persephone are frequently invoked together or treated as manifestations of the same divine power. PGM IV.2785-2890 contains a spell addressing 'Persephone-Hekate, goddess of three ways and three faces', explicitly connecting their identities.

The philosopher Porphyry (3rd century CE) offers theoretical justification for their connection in *On Images*, explaining that 'Persephone, who oversees all that grows and dies, and Hekate, who presides over transitions, share authority over the cycles of life and death'. This philosophical interpretation suggests conceptual reasons for the goddesses' association beyond mere coincidence of cult.

Hekate and Selene/Luna

Hekate's connection with lunar deities became increasingly prominent during the Hellenistic and Roman periods, culminating in explicit identifications with Selene (Greek) and Luna (Roman).

This association emphasised Hekate's nocturnal aspects and her governance over magical operations conducted under moonlight. Literary evidence for this connection appears clearly in Apollonius Rhodius' *Argonautica* (3rd century BCE), which describes Medea sacrificing to 'Hekate Brimo, daughter of Perseus, who governs the night'. This reference connects Hekate to Selene through shared mythology, as Perseus was traditionally considered Selene's father. Archaeological evidence includes Hellenistic and Roman-era amulets and gems depicting Hekate with explicit lunar iconography. The British Museum holds several 2nd–3rd century CE magical gems showing Hekate with a crescent moon crown and the inscription ΣΕΛΗΝΗ-ΕΚΑΤΗ (Selene-Hekate), confirming the formal recognition of their unified identity. The name Nyktipolos (Night-Wanderer) was applied to both goddesses, as seen in inscriptions and magical texts. A notable example comes from a 2nd century CE altar found near Rome dedicated to Luna-Hekate Nyktipolos, demonstrating the Roman adoption of this designation. In Apuleius' *Metamorphoses* (2nd century CE), the goddess Isis claims Hekate and Luna among her many identities, stating: 'The Ephesians call me Diana [Artemis]... others Proserpine [Persephone], others Hekate, and still others Luna.'

In the Roman period, the cult of Selene and lunar aspects of Diana (the Roman equivalent of Artemis) are attested in epigraphic evidence from various Cypriot cities. An inscription from Amathus dating to the 2nd century CE mentions a dedication to Diana Lucifera (Light-bearing Diana).

Hekate and Isis
The connection between Hekate and the Egyptian goddess Isis developed primarily during the Hellenistic period, when Greek and Egyptian religious traditions intermingled. This syncretism emphasised both goddesses' associations with magic, wisdom, and protective functions.

Excavations at Alexandria have revealed 2nd–1st century BCE terracotta figurines depicting a triple-formed goddess with attributes of both Hekate (torches, keys) and Isis (sistrum, Isiac knot), suggesting popular recognition of their connected identities. A bilingual Greek-Demotic inscription from 1st century BCE Memphis addresses Isis-Hekate Polyonymos, recognising their multiple identities and overlapping domains. The PGM contain several spells invoking Isis-Hekate as a unified divine power, particularly for magical operations involving transformation and protection.

Hekate and Enodia

The connection between Hekate and the Thessalian goddess Enodia represents a different type of divine association; it is less a syncretism than a case of regional variation or possible original identity. While 'Enodia' later became merely an epithet of Hekate, evidence suggests that in Thessaly, Enodia may have been an independent deity who gradually merged with the more widely worshipped Hekate. Literary evidence for this connection appears in Sophocles' fragment 535 (5th century BCE), where Enodia is described with attributes typically associated with Hekate. Additionally, Aristophanes' fragment 515 mentions Enodia Hekate, suggesting either a compound deity or the process of syncretism already underway. Archaeological evidence from Thessaly provides the clearest picture of this relationship. Excavations at Pherae have yielded numerous 5th–4th century BCE dedications to Enodia alone, without reference to Hekate. However, later inscriptions (3rd–2nd century BCE) from the same region increasingly use Enodia Hekate or Hekate Enodia, suggesting a gradual merging of identities. Shared iconography provides further evidence of their connection. Several 4th century BCE Thessalian coins depict a goddess with torch and dogs, which are attributes associated with both Enodia and Hekate, demonstrating their visual similarity or deliberate identification.

The Archaeological Museum of Volos houses multiple votive reliefs showing this iconographic overlap. The philosopher Porphyry (3rd century CE) explicitly addresses this connection in *On Abstinence*, noting that 'the Thessalians sacrifice black female puppies to Enodia, whom others call Hekate'. This passage confirms that by the Roman period, the identification was widely recognised, though with awareness of its regional origins.

Hekate and Cybele/Magna Mater
Hekate's association with the Anatolian mother goddess Cybele (known to Romans as Magna Mater) developed primarily in Asia Minor, where both goddesses had strong cult presences. Their connection emphasised shared attributes of liminality, wild nature, and ecstatic worship. Literary evidence appears in fragments of the Roman scholar Marcus Terentius Varro's writings (1st century BCE), preserved by Augustine, which mention that Romans sometimes identified Hekate with aspects of the 'Great Mother'. Similarly, Diodorus Siculus (1st century BCE) notes connections between Hekate's Corybantes and Cybele's Galli priests, suggesting parallel cult practices. Archaeological evidence comes primarily from sites in western Asia Minor. Excavations at Lagina revealed architectural elements incorporating iconography associated with Cybele, including lions and tympana.

These syncretistic elements suggest deliberate efforts to emphasise connections between the goddesses within Hekate's primary cult centre. The shared designation Despoina (Mistress) appears in inscriptions for both goddesses. A notable 2nd century CE dedication from Phrygia addresses Hekate-Cybele Despoina, confirming their formal cultic connection. The fusion became particularly pronounced during the Roman Imperial period.

Medea and Hekate
Medea's relationship with Hekate is fundamental to understanding Medea's character and power. Hekate was Medea's patron goddess and, in some accounts, her mother or ancestor. In Apollonius of Rhodes' *Argonautica*, Medea is explicitly described as a priestess of Hekate, tending her temple in Colchis. Her magical abilities were based on her knowledge of potions, herbs, and incantations which derive from her connection to Hekate. When preparing to help Jason, Medea invokes Hekate and performs rituals dedicated to the goddess. In Euripides' play *Medea*, she invokes Hekate as 'the mistress I revere above all others, my chosen helper, Hekate, who dwells in the inner chamber of my house.' This intimate relationship suggests that Medea's magical powers are channelled through her devotion to the goddess. The archaeological record provides context for this relationship.

Cult sites dedicated to Hekate have been found throughout the ancient Greek world, including areas around the Black Sea coast. Votive offerings and inscriptions suggest that Hekate was worshipped in regions associated with the historical Colchis.

These associations are not merely theoretical but manifest in practical worship through shared sanctuaries, priesthoods, iconography and epithets. This illustrates that divine connections existed at multiple levels, in official cult, philosophical interpretation, magical practice, and personal devotion. Hekate's identity extended far beyond her individual cult. Academic studies of Hecate's origins reflect broader developments in the study of ancient Mediterranean religion. Archaeological discoveries, particularly at the Lagina sanctuary, led to reassessments of Hecate's Anatolian significance. Today, the evidence from Caria compels us to view Hecate not as a minor foreign deity absorbed into Greek cult and religious practices, but as a major Anatolian goddess whose character has evolved through Hellenic interpretation and worship. For me, the issue is not from where did Hekate originate? But how do her energies, qualities and designations impact on my personal journey and magickal practices, and where and how do I make the connections that guide my daily rituals and work?

The exploration of Hekate within the divine feminine pantheon illuminates her position as both independent deity and collaborative force. For me, her relationships with Artemis, Persephone, and Demeter demonstrate that spiritual maturity involves understanding how individual power can enhance rather than diminish collective wisdom. The divine feminine emerges not as a competition between goddesses but as a web of interconnected energies, each supporting and strengthening the whole.

HEKATE'S BOTANICALS

Diodorus Siculus in his Bibliotheca Historica (1st century BCE), describes Hekate as being ingenious in mixing deadly poisons and discovering aconite. Diodorus also describes that Hekate had two daughters, who we know as Circe and Medea, although in other accounts with different lineage. Medea is often described as a priestess of, not necessarily daughter of Hekate. Both Circe and Medea are renown for their craft with pharmacopeia and botanicals. Of Circe, Diodorus writes,

"Compounding of all sorts of medicines, found out the wonderful natures and efficacy of diverse sorts of roots and herbs, many of them learnt of her Mother Hecate"

The Orphic Argonautica (c. 4th-5th century CE) describes a Garden of Hekate in Colchis, the home of Medea, which contained aconite, mandrake, and other powerful plants. This sacred grove was described as containing amongst others, laurels, cornels, plane trees, asphodel, verbena, sage, mandrake, dittany, saffron, white hellebore, aconite, and many other plants with powerful characteristics. Ovid in Metamorphoses describes Pallas Athena sprinkling Arachne with drugs of Hekate (Hecateidos herbae), which transformed the girl into a spider.

Archaeological discoveries from sanctuaries associated with her worship have revealed charred plant remains, residues on curse tablets, and offerings deposited at crossroads, providing material evidence that practitioners understood plants not merely as ingredients but as allies in navigating the liminal spaces Hekate commands (Johnston, 1999). Each botanical choice reflected sophisticated knowledge where a plant's physical properties, its toxicity, aroma, appearance, and growing conditions corresponded to particular aspects of her multifaceted nature. From deadly aconite gathered under specific lunar phases to protective garlic left at crossroads during the dark moon, these plants served as bridges between the mundane and sacred, the cultivated and wild, the healing and harmful.

This chapter explores the botanicals most intimately connected with Hekate's worship, examining their characteristics, historical uses, and significance within her ritual framework. Understanding these plants offers more than historical insight; it opens pathways for contemporary practice, particularly for those of us drawn to cultivate these living connections in our own gardens and sacred spaces.

For modern practitioners seeking to create their own garden, here is a summary of some of the plants most commonly associated with Hekate:

Aconite (Aconitum napellus) commonly known as monkshood or wolfsbane, is an herbaceous perennial belonging to the Ranunculaceae family (same as buttercups). It grows to approximately 1–1.5 metres in height, featuring deeply lobed, palmate dark green leaves and distinctive hooded flowers that bloom in late summer to early autumn. These flowers are a deep violet-blue colour, with a helmet or hood-like shape that gives rise to the common name 'monkshood'. The plant produces seed-bearing follicles after flowering. All parts of aconite contain the potent alkaloid aconitine, making it one of the most toxic plants in the European flora. Its poison affects the nervous system and heart, causing numbness, paralysis, and potentially death, even in small doses.

This extreme toxicity contributed significantly to its magical associations and ritual applications in antiquity. As the name Wolfsbane suggests, it was apparently used in Greece to poison the wolf populations. Aconite prefers cool, moist conditions and humus-rich, well-drained soils with consistent moisture. It grows best in partial shade with rich, moist but well-drained soil.

Propagation is typically achieved through seeds sown in autumn, or by division of the tuberous roots in spring or autumn when the plant is dormant. However, handling these roots requires exceptional caution due to the potential for dermal absorption of toxins.

Aconite appears in several significant contexts associated with Hekate. In a ritual for dream divination, practitioners are instructed to 'take the root of aconite, ground finely, and mix with rose oil' to create an anointing unguent for the temples before sleep. This application, whilst dangerous by modern understanding, was believed to facilitate communication with Hekate through dream states. In another lengthy invocation to Hekate, aconite is mentioned as a component of fumigation: 'Burn aconite leaves gathered at the dark moon, mixed with sulphur and pine resin.' The smoke produced was believed to create a chthonic atmosphere conducive to manifesting Hekate's presence during nocturnal rites. Aconite also appears in protective amulets associated with Hekatean magic. Such as the 'the root of aconite wrapped in black wool, which was carried during dangerous magical operations involving underworld powers. The amulet was believed to provide protection through sympathetic magic, with the deadly plant serving as a ward against other deadly forces.

The preparation of aconite for ritual use required specific protocols. Such as aconite should be 'gathered when the moon is in Scorpio, without casting a shadow upon it' highlighting the astrological considerations governing magical herbalism in antiquity.

Other practices include aconite as particularly potent for necromantic operations, with curse tablets associated with Hekate. One binding spell includes the instruction to 'inscribe the names upon lead with a bronze stylus dipped in aconite juice'. The toxic nature of the plant was believed to lend additional power to maledictions performed under Hekate's authority. The extreme danger posed by aconite contributed to its restricted use in Hekatean rituals. Only initiated practitioners with specific knowledge would have employed the plant, and its use marked particularly serious magical operations.

Belladonna (Atropa belladonna) Various nightshades appear prominently in Hekatean formulae, particularly in spells for vision, transformation and communion with spirits. The term 'nightshade' can refer to several plants in the Solanaceae family, most commonly Atropa belladonna (deadly nightshade) and Solanum nigrum (black nightshade).

Atropa belladonna, famously known for dilating the pupils was used by Italian women to make them more alluring. It was also likely to be one of the ingredients in aqua Tofana, a slow-acting poison sold as 'Manna di San Nicola' in Renaissance Italy, disguised as either a devotional flask or cosmetics. It is a perennial herbaceous plant, growing 0.5–1.5 metres tall with ovate leaves and bell-shaped purple-brown flowers that develop into glossy black berries. The entire plant contains tropane alkaloids, making it both medicinally valuable and potentially lethal. Archaeological evidence from several ancient sites has revealed nightshade seeds in contexts that suggest deliberate cultivation and use. A spell for divine revelation explicitly calls for nightshade as part of a complex ritual: 'Take frankincense kernels [and] also put nightshade juice on them. Then at night, when the goddess is at the full, in her power, and appears in her full brightness, offer the frankincense kernels in a new censer'.

The incorporation of nightshade into Hekatean rituals reflects several significant properties. Its psychoactive effects were valued for inducing altered states of consciousness associated with divine communion. Most importantly, nightshade was believed to facilitate communication with spirits and deities, making it particularly appropriate for theurgic operations seeking direct contact with Hekate.

Black Cumin (Nigella sativa) appears in several Hekatean spells and rituals such as being an ingredient of a complex fumigation offering to Hekate: 'Take storax, myrrh, sage, frankincense, a fruit seed, and black cumin all in equal measure and pound them together with a hawk's heart.'

It also is used in protective amulets and conjurations. Nigella sativa is an annual flowering plant growing 20–60 centimetres tall with finely divided, thread-like leaves. Its most distinctive features are its pale blue or white flowers with elaborate structures and the inflated capsules that develop after flowering, containing numerous small, angular, black seeds. These seeds have a pungent aroma somewhat reminiscent of black pepper mixed with oregano and have a slightly bitter taste. It is native to southern Europe, North Africa, and Southwest Asia. It grows well in open fields and disturbed ground, often appearing in agricultural margins and fallow fields.

In antiquity, it was both harvested from wild populations and intentionally cultivated for culinary, medicinal and magical purposes. Cultivation is relatively straightforward, with seeds sown directly in well-drained soil during spring. The plants mature within three to four months, producing seed capsules that are harvested when fully dried on the stem.

Archaeological evidence from several ancient Egyptian sites has revealed black cumin seeds in storage vessels, indicating its deliberate cultivation and preservation. There is some archaeological evidence that supports the magical use of black cumin in contexts associated with Hekate worship, where analysis of residues from several curse tablets has revealed traces of organic material consistent with Nigella sativa, suggesting its incorporation into binding spells performed under Hekate's authority.

Cypress (Cupressus sempervirens) I have ambitions to plant a small Cypress tree near my dark moon garden. With its dark, evergreen foliage and distinctive silhouette, it is still strongly associated with death, mourning and the underworld in ancient Greek culture. The Mediterranean cypress was widely cultivated throughout Greece, Rome, and the Near East, particularly in cemeteries and sacred groves associated with chthonic deities. It thrives in hot, dry conditions with good drainage and full sun exposure. Medicinally, cypress had limited but significant applications. Dioscorides notes that cypress cones, mixed with myrrh and wine, were effective against dysentery and urinary disorders. The bark and leaves were used to treat haemorrhoids and varicose veins, due to their astringent properties.

In magical practices associated with Hekate, cypress branches were used to decorate altars and sacred spaces during rituals. The tree's association with the underworld made it particularly appropriate for necromantic rituals and communications with the dead. Archaeological evidence from several sanctuaries has revealed charred cypress wood, suggesting its use in ritual fires.

Dandelion (Taraxacum officinale) The common dandelion aligns with many aspects of Hekatean magic, particularly in the realm of divination and spirit communication. It is a perennial herbaceous plant growing from a sturdy taproot. It forms a rosette of deeply toothed leaves (the name 'dandelion' derives from the French 'dent de lion' or 'lion's tooth') from which emerge hollow stems bearing solitary yellow flower heads. These mature into the distinctive spherical seed heads composed of numerous achenes, each attached to a feathery pappus that enables wind dispersal. The entire plant contains a milky latex that exudes when stems or leaves are broken. When we were children, this sap was understood to make you wet the bed. As it is a diuretic, there was at least an element of truth in the idea. Although we also believed that eating apple pips meant an apple tree would grow in your stomach. Fortunately, I have no evidence of this to be true.

In antiquity, dandelion was both gathered from wild populations and semi-cultivated in garden settings. Archaeological evidence suggests that dandelions were grown in designated areas of ancient gardens, particularly those associated with healing sanctuaries and temples where medicinal plants were cultivated. There are few examples of ancient direct links to Hekate, but blowing the clocks has the potential as a form of aeromancy, connecting to Hekate's oracular aspects. The clocks represent the moon, whilst the bright yellow flowers, the sun. This duality made it appropriate for rituals invoking Hekate in her role as a messenger/traveller between worlds, with lunar associations, the transformation of the dandelion's yellow flower to white seed head parallels lunar phases, connecting it to Hekate's lunar aspects. Several spell and ritual formulae texts mention 'moon herbs' in connection with Hekate, which some believe may have included dandelion. The dandelion's mild bitter principles and diuretic effects were believed to assist in purification before magical operations, which is a common requirement in rituals dedicated to Hekate.

Dill (Anethum graveolens) is an annual herb growing 40–150 centimetres tall with hollow stems and finely divided, feathery leaves that emit a distinctive sweet, aromatic scent when crushed.

The plant produces umbrella-shaped clusters of small yellow flowers that develop into flat, oval seeds with pronounced ridges. Both the leaves and seeds contain volatile oils responsible for dill's characteristic aroma and flavour. Native to the eastern Mediterranean and western Asia, dill thrives in sunny locations with well-drained soil. It grows naturally in open fields, disturbed ground and agricultural margins throughout the Mediterranean basin. In antiquity, dill was both harvested from wild populations and deliberately cultivated for culinary, medicinal and magical purposes. Cultivation is straightforward, with seeds sown directly in well-drained soil during spring. The plants mature rapidly, producing harvestable leaves within six to eight weeks and seeds within three to four months. Dill is connected to lunar deities, strengthening its association with Hekate in her lunar aspect. Dill appears in several Hekatean formulae particularly in protective and purification rituals. I grow dill in my herb garden rather than the moon garden. A divination ritual dedicated to Hekate explicitly mentions dill as part of a protective measure: 'Take dill and nightshade and a little crab's foot and grind them together... use this as an ointment upon your body when you are about to receive the divine essence.'

Dittany of Crete (Origanum dictamnus) is a plant native to Crete and was strongly associated with both healing and magical practices in Hekate's worship. According to Virgil's Aeneid, Venus gathered dittany from Cretan mountains to heal Aeneas's wounds, establishing its reputation as a powerful healing herb. The plant was primarily cultivated in Crete, growing on the limestone slopes of Mount Dicte — a location with significant mythological importance. Dittany requires well-drained soil and sunny conditions and was carefully harvested due to its relative scarcity. Today in Crete it is a protected plant, although it is possible to buy it from reputable garden centres and nurseries. I have a dittany in my garden. Medicinally, dittany was renowned for its antimicrobial and wound-healing properties. Hippocrates recommended it for treating wounds and ulcers, while Dioscorides noted its effectiveness in expelling splinters and arrowheads from wounds — perhaps the origin of Virgil's reference (Dioscorides, trans. 2000, 3.32).

In magical practices associated with Hekate, dittany was burned as incense to facilitate trancework and divination. Its strong aromatic properties were believed to create an atmosphere conducive to communication with spirits and deities.

Archaeological evidence from several sanctuaries associated with Hekate has revealed burnt remnants of plant material consistent with Dittany.

Frankincense (Boswellia sacra/carterii) is mentioned frequently as an offering to Hekate, particularly in rituals requiring her benevolent aspects. Frankincense comes from small trees of the genus Boswellia, typically standing 2–8 metres tall with papery, peeling bark and compound leaves arranged in opposite pairs.

The trees have a gnarled, twisted appearance due to their growth in harsh environments. The distinctively aromatic resin is harvested from incisions made in the trunk, from which a milky-white sap leaks and hardens into teardrops of various sizes and colours ranging from pale yellow to amber.

Frankincense trees grow primarily in the southern Arabian Peninsula (particularly Oman and Yemen) and in northeast Africa (Somalia and Ethiopia). They thrive in arid, rocky conditions with little rainfall, often clinging to limestone cliffs and rocky outcrops. The trees are not cultivated in plantations but rather managed in their wild state by local communities who have harvested them for generations.

Although not native to the Mediterranean, frankincense was extensively imported into Greece and Egypt through well-established trade routes, making it readily available in magical and religious contexts throughout the ancient world.

Archaeological evidence from shipwrecks has revealed significant quantities of frankincense being transported across the Mediterranean as early as the 14th century BCE. One spell used for divine revelation specifically calls for frankincense as an offering to Hekate-Selene: 'Take frankincense kernels, put nightshade juice on them. Then at night, when the goddess is at the full, in her power, and appears in her full brightness, offer the frankincense kernels in a new censer.'

Unlike many other plants associated with Hekate's darker aspects, frankincense was particularly associated with her celestial and lunar manifestations. There are several invocations to Hekate-Selene, emphasising the goddess's connection to the full moon. The ritual burning of frankincense was believed to create a bridge between earthly and divine realms, making it particularly suitable for theurgic practices seeking divine communion rather than the commanding of spirits more common in necromantic rites.

Garlic (Allium sativum) though less dramatic than some of Hekate's other botanical associations, garlic held significant importance in her worship. It was a key component of the Deipnon of Hekate, and offerings were left at crossroads during the dark of the moon. This ritual is explained in Chapter 4. Garlic is widely cultivated throughout the Mediterranean region, being one of the oldest known cultivated plants in the area. Archaeological evidence suggests its cultivation in Greece dates back to at least the Bronze Age. Garlic appears frequently in rituals associated with Hekate, particularly in protective (apotropaic) contexts.

Allium sativum is a bulbous perennial plant growing 30–90 centimetres tall. It produces a single erect stem bearing flat, elongated leaves and, in some varieties, a terminal flowering head containing small, greenish-white flowers. Each clove contains potent volatile compounds that produce garlic's characteristic pungent aroma and taste when damaged.

Wild ancestors of garlic originated in Central Asia and were widespread throughout the Mediterranean region. It thrives in well-drained, fertile soils with full sun exposure, making it well-suited to the agricultural practices of ancient Greece and Egypt.

Archaeological evidence suggests extensive garlic cultivation throughout the Mediterranean basin from at least the Bronze Age onwards. Cultivation involves planting individual cloves in autumn or early spring, with each clove developing into a completely new bulb by mid-summer.

Medicinally, garlic was one of the most versatile plants in the ancient pharmacopoeia. Hippocrates recommended it for a wide range of conditions, from respiratory ailments to parasitic infections. Dioscorides noted its warming properties and effectiveness against intestinal parasites. In magical practices associated with Hekate, garlic served a dual purpose. It was both an offering to the goddess and a protective agent against harmful spirits. Garlic bulbs have been discovered at archaeological sites associated with Hekate worship, particularly at crossroads where offerings would have been left. I grow lots of garlic around the moon garden and love the big heads of flowers in the early summer.

Hellebores (Helleborus Niger) Both black and white hellebore were strongly associated with Hekate's magical practices. I have black hellebores in my dark moon garden and the white in the moon garden.

According to myth, Melampus used hellebore to cure the madness of King Proetus's daughters, establishing its connection with mental states and purification, both domains over which Hekate has influence. Hellebores prefer partial shade and rich, moist soils.

Medicinally, hellebore was primarily used as a purgative and to treat mental disorders. Hippocrates prescribed it for cases of mania and melancholy, while Theophrastus notes its effectiveness in treating epilepsy. However, the plant's toxicity was well-recognised, with Dioscorides cautioning about appropriate dosages.

In magical practices, hellebore is particularly associated with purification rituals dedicated to Hekate. The Orphic Hymn to Hekate refers to her as 'tomb spirit' and 'delighting in purifications', contexts in which hellebore would have been employed.

Laurel (Laurus nobilis) appears frequently in rituals associated with Hekate, particularly in divinatory and oracular contexts. Laurus nobilis is an aromatic evergreen tree growing 10–18 metres tall, with glossy, dark green, leathery leaves that release a distinctive scent when crushed. The tree produces small yellow flowers that develop into black, berry-like fruits containing a single seed.

Both the leaves and berries contain essential oils responsible for laurel's characteristic aroma. Native to the Mediterranean region, laurel thrives in the mild, humid conditions of coastal areas and low mountain slopes. It grows naturally in woodland margins and sheltered valleys throughout Greece, Italy, and the Levant.

In antiquity, laurel was both harvested from wild populations and deliberately cultivated, particularly around temples and sacred sites associated with Apollo and other oracular deities. The trees grow relatively slowly but can live for centuries when properly established. My laurel is more than two metres high and a few years ago survived three nights of minus 19 degrees Celsius, which killed off a 45-year-old Olive tree.

One invocation to Hekate includes laurel as part of a ritual preparation: 'Take laurel leaves and pulverize them; smear them on your lips with honey while invoking the goddess.' The incorporation of laurel into Hekatean rituals reflects its strong associations with prophecy and divination. While primarily associated with Apollo in mainstream Greek religion, laurel's divinatory properties made it equally valuable in Hekatean magical practices focused on revelation and prophecy.

Mandrake (Mandragora officinarum) appears in several Hekatean formulae within the PGM, particularly in conjurations and dream-sending rituals. Mandragora officinarum is a perennial herbaceous plant with a distinctive large, forked taproot that sometimes resembles a human figure — a feature that contributed significantly to its magical reputation. The plant grows as a rosette of large, wrinkled, ovate leaves lying flat against the ground, from which emerge small, bell-shaped flowers ranging from purple to greenish white. These flowers develop into yellow berries containing numerous small seeds.

The entire plant contains tropane alkaloids, making it both medicinally valuable and potentially toxic. Native to lands surrounding the Mediterranean Sea, mandrake grows naturally in rocky, semi-shaded areas with well-drained calcareous soils. It typically appears in abandoned fields, olive groves, and the edges of woodland areas from Spain to Syria. In antiquity, while some mandrake was harvested from wild populations, evidence suggests deliberate cultivation, particularly in Egypt and Greece.

Cultivation of mandrake is challenging due to its slow growth and specific requirements. The plant is propagated from seeds, which require a period of cold stratification before germination. Once established, mandrake plants can live for many years, gradually developing the large taproot that was so valued in magical operations.

Myrrh (Commiphora myrrha) also features prominently in Hekatean rituals, often paired with other resins like frankincense and storax. Myrrh has a long association with magical practices, commonly its used for cleansing a sanctified space, consecrating magical tools and in protection spells. It was often used as an offering to the goddesses and gods, and Egyptians also used it in mumification rites.

Myrrh has many traditional medicinal uses, from chapped lips to anti-carcinogenic uses, for which modern science is still playing catch-up. Commiphora myrrha is a thorny shrub. Its most distinctive feature is its ability to produce an aromatic oleo-gum-resin when the bark is wounded. The resin appears as yellowish-white droplets that harden and darken upon exposure to air, eventually forming reddish-brown lumps with a bitter, medicinal taste and distinctive earthy, slightly musky aroma. Myrrh trees grow naturally in the dry, rocky hillsides of northeast Africa (primarily Somalia and Ethiopia) and the Arabian Peninsula. They are highly adapted to arid conditions, requiring minimal rainfall and well-drained soils.

Like frankincense, myrrh was not typically cultivated in formal plantations but rather harvested from wild stands by local communities with generational knowledge of sustainable collection methods. Myrrh reached the Mediterranean world through established trade routes crossing the Red Sea and Arabian Peninsula, becoming a valuable commodity in Egyptian, Greek and later Roman markets.

Archaeological evidence from port cities like Alexandria has revealed significant quantities of myrrh imported for religious, magical and medicinal purposes.

In PGM IV.2708-2784, a divination ritual dedicated to Hekate explicitly calls for myrrh as both an offering and an ingredient in ritual ink: 'Take myrrh and write with it on a leaf from a persea tree; write the formula while saying it.' The ritual continues with instructions to burn the leaf while reciting an invocation to Hekate. The use of myrrh in Hekatean rituals serves multiple purposes. As an ingredient in ritual ink, it provides a magically charged medium for inscribing divine names and formulae. Most significantly, myrrh was associated with preservation and transitions between states. There are at least 21 references to Myrrh in the PGM corpus

Pennyroyal (Mentha pulegium) appears several times within the PGM, particularly in purification rituals and protection spells. It is also a key ingredient in Kykeon as described in the Iliad and Hymn to Demeter. Mentha pulegium is a small perennial herb growing 10--30 centimetres tall with creeping stems that root at the nodes. It bears small, oval leaves arranged in opposite pairs along square stems, a characteristic feature of the mint family. The leaves are distinctively aromatic, releasing a strong, minty scent when crushed. During summer, the plant produces whorls of small purple or lilac flowers arranged in dense clusters. I grow pennyroyal, but not in the moon garden but in my herb garden.

Pennyroyal grows naturally throughout the Mediterranean region, particularly in damp areas such as stream banks, marsh edges, and seasonally wet meadows. Unlike many plants associated with Hekate, it prefers moist soil conditions rather than dry, rocky terrain. It was both gathered from wild stands and cultivated in garden settings throughout the ancient world, spreading readily through both seeds and creeping stems. The plant's vigorous growth habit allows for multiple harvests throughout the growing season, with fresh growth quickly replacing cut stems.

Pinecones (Pinus spp.) appear in several contexts within the PGM, and broader magical traditions associated with Hekate, particularly in purification rituals and as symbolic representations of the torch, one of Hekate's primary attributes. They are woody, scaled structures that develop from female cones, taking two to three years to mature. The stone pine produces large, rounded cones up to 15 centimetres in length containing edible seeds (pine nuts), while the Aleppo pine produces smaller, more elongated cones. Both species produce resinous substances with distinctive aromatic properties. Pine trees are widespread throughout the Mediterranean region, growing in various habitats from coastal areas to mountain slopes. Pinus pinea typically grows in coastal regions with sandy soils and was deliberately cultivated around sanctuaries and sacred groves. Cultivation of pine trees involves seed propagation, with trees growing relatively slowly but living for centuries when properly established. I am fortunate in having a very large and old pine in my garden, that provides shade to some of the plants in the dark moon garden.

In PGM IV.2708–2784, a divination ritual that invokes Hekate mentions 'pine wood' as part of the ritual apparatus: 'Let there be nearby a tripod of pine wood and a raw clay lamp which you will light.'

While this does not explicitly mention pinecones, the ritual significance of pine in Hekatean contexts is clear. More broadly, pinecones feature in several ways in rituals associated with Hekate. Pinecones were used as sprinklers for lustral water in purification rituals. Their complex structure allowed them to hold and disperse water effectively, while their resinous nature added aromatic properties to the water. Purification was a common preliminary step in rituals dedicated to Hekate. Pinecones were used as the heads of torches due to their flammable resinous nature, connecting them directly to Hekate's iconography, as she is frequently depicted holding torches that illuminate the darkness and guide the way at crossroads. In Greek funerary contexts, pinecones symbolised eternal life and regeneration. This connected them to Hekate's role as a psychopomp guiding souls through the underworld. Several PGM texts mention 'fruits of the earth' in funerary contexts that scholars believe included pinecones. Pinecones topped the thyrsus; a staff associated with mystery cults and ecstatic rituals. While primarily connected to Dionysian worship, the thyrsus also appears in some magical contexts associated with Hekate, particularly in rituals involving altered states of consciousness. The Dionysian connection of pinecones creates an interesting intersection with Hekate veneration.

Sage (Salvia spp.) appears in several Hekatean formulae within the PGM, particularly in fumigations and protective spells. The term 'sage' in the PGM refers to various species of Salvia native to the Mediterranean region, most commonly Salvia officinalis or Salvia triloba. These are aromatic perennial shrubs growing 30–60 centimetres tall with woody stems, grey-green textured leaves and whorls of purple-blue flowers that bloom in late spring. The leaves are distinctively aromatic, containing volatile oils that produce a strong, camphoraceous scent when crushed.

In Piemonte Italy, we batter and deep fry sage leaves in the spring when they are young and delicious. Mediterranean sage species grow naturally throughout Greece, Turkey and the Balkan region, typically flourishing in dry, rocky soils with full sun exposure. They are drought-resistant plants that thrive in the harsh conditions of Mediterranean hillsides and coastal areas. Sage was both gathered from wild populations and cultivated in garden settings throughout the ancient world.

Cultivation requires well-drained soil and minimal watering, making sage relatively easy to grow in the Mediterranean climate. In the PGM IV corpus sage appears at least four times.

The properties that made sage valuable in Hekatean rituals included its strong aromatic qualities and its reputation for purification and protection. The plant's association with wisdom (reflected in its Latin name Salvia, derived from 'salvare' meaning 'to heal' or 'to save', also connected it to Hekate's aspect as a goddess of divine knowledge and magical wisdom. Archaeological evidence from several temples and sacred sites has revealed charred remains of plant material consistent with sage, suggesting its widespread use in ritual fumigations throughout the ancient Mediterranean.

Storax (Styrax officinalis) appears prominently in rituals throughout the PGM. Styrax officinalis is a deciduous shrub or small tree growing 3–5 metres tall with a spreading crown. Its most distinctive feature is its clusters of white, bell-shaped flowers that bloom in late spring, exuding a sweet, vanilla-like fragrance. The bark, when wounded, produces a resinous exudate that hardens into the aromatic gum known as storax. Native to the eastern Mediterranean region, storax thrives in dry, rocky hillsides throughout Greece, Turkey, Syria and the Levant. It prefers well-drained soils and full sun exposure, often growing amongst other Mediterranean scrubland vegetation. In antiquity, the collection of storax resin was a specialised practice.

Harvesters would carefully make incisions in the bark during summer months, returning later to collect the hardened resin.

Thyme (Thymus vulgaris) Beyond its culinary applications, thyme is commonly used by magickal practitioners. It possesses protective properties; it wards off negative energies and is used in rituals for purification and to attract health and healing.

Its versatile nature makes thyme a staple herb in both kitchen pantries and sacred spaces alike, bridging the mundane and the magical with its potent essence. Thyme provides a sense of direction for the soul, and this is probably another reason why Greek soldiers took it into battle. Not only did it increase their physical energy, but it was thought to enhance the mental and spiritual understanding they needed to follow their destiny and vision. Apart from magickal work, I use it to make 'flu bombs' to ward off winter viruses.

The recipe is hot water, lemon juice, a sprig of thyme, a sprig of rosemary, a small piece of fresh ginger and garlic. If you need to sweeten it, a teaspoon of maple syrup helps. Drink it three times a day for three days at the onset of any nasty cold/flu-type virus.

Wormwood (Artemisia absinthium) is evident in several Hekatean formulae within the PGM, particularly in protective and banishing rituals. Artemisia absinthium is a perennial herbaceous plant growing 30–100 centimetres tall with silvery-grey, deeply divided leaves that emit an intensely bitter aroma when crushed. The plant produces small, yellow-green flowers arranged in nodding clusters along branched stems. All parts contain thujone and other bitter compounds responsible for wormwood's characteristic intense bitterness and its medicinal and psychoactive properties. Native to temperate regions of Europe, Asia, and North Africa, wormwood thrives in dry, rocky soils with full sun exposure. It grows naturally in wastelands roadsides, and disturbed ground throughout the Mediterranean basin.

In ancient times, wormwood was both harvested from wild populations and deliberately cultivated for medicinal and magical purposes. Cultivation is relatively straightforward, with plants propagated from either seeds or root divisions. Once established, wormwood is drought-tolerant and requires minimal maintenance.

The inclusion of wormwood in Hekatean rituals stems from several significant properties. Its intense bitterness repels evil spirits and negative influences, making it valuable in protective magic. Wormwood's mild psychoactive properties were believed to enhance visionary experiences, making it used for divinatory rituals under Hekate's authority. I use it, amongst other things, for dream working.

Yew Trees (Taxus baccate) have strong associations with Hekate in her chthonic aspect. According to Pliny the Elder's Natural History, the yew has 'the most sinister associations and is considered a deadly omen'. I have an English Yew in my woodland garden. They are cultivated throughout Europe, although almost reached extinction due to the demand of the wood to make long bows for the English in the Hundred Years' War.

Yew was particularly significant in sacred groves associated with death and the underworld. The trees were often planted in cemeteries and around temples dedicated to Hekate and other chthonic deities. The berries, bark and needles of the yew contain taxine alkaloids, which have potent cardiotoxic effects. Despite this toxicity, the yew had some medicinal applications in antiquity. Celsus mentions its use in treatments for snake bites, though he acknowledges its dangerous properties.

In magical contexts, yew was associated with necromancy and communicating with the dead — practices over which Hekate presided. Wands made from yew wood were believed to facilitate movement between worlds.

These plants share more than their association with Hekate, they reveal patterns in how ancient practitioners understood her nature. Many thrive in liminal spaces such as woodland edges, disturbed ground, rocky hillsides, mirroring Hekate's own position at boundaries and thresholds. Their properties span extremes, capable of healing or harming, revealing or concealing, protecting or cursing, embodying the paradoxes inherent in the goddess herself. Growing these plants creates living links to historical practice whilst grounding abstract knowledge in soil, season, and the daily rhythms of tending. As I have discovered through my own journey, working with Hekate's botanicals transforms understanding from an intellectual exercise into embodied practice, literally from the dirt to the divine. The transition from reading about these plants to growing them, from studying ancient texts to standing in a garden at twilight, marks a threshold crossing of its own, and one that leads us into the more personal territory of creating sacred space, where theory meets earth and historical devotion meets contemporary experience.

CREATING A MOON GARDEN

In 2018 I had the urge to build a moon garden. This came out of nowhere but felt like a shove in the back. It took me the best part of two years to ignore it before considering where to place it. I staked it out in the grounds of our old farmhouse several times, before it became absolutely obvious where it needed to be. Whilst we were excavating the space, the only thing we found was an old key. As if that was not enough of sign, in the garden there was already a Strophalos. It had been staring at me for years before I ever made the connection. My moon garden now consists of six beds, an altar space and a Strophalos.

The garden was conceived as a sacred space, to venerate the divine feminine that is both related to lunar power but also continues the tradition of magical botanical practices. The original idea was to grow only white and night-related flowers. Because of my cultural traditions, I decided to use British and some Cypriot moon references in the construction and planting within the moon garden.

In my garden there are flowering plants for each month. In winter there is a winter-flowering cherry, *Helleborus natale,* white cyclamen, *Chrysanthemum,* Saccoccia, *Camelia aconite.* In spring: white periwinkle, *Hydrangea,* white wisteria, *Anemone, Viburnum* Geranium macrorrhizum, *Cerastium tomentosum,* Abelia, and peony. During summer: *Gaura, Echinacea, Philadelphus (Saxifragaceae) Agapanthus, Lilium* 'Muscat', honeysuckle, *Artemisia absinthe, Artemisia vulgaris,* white Roses, white strawberries. Finally, in Autumn: *Sedum spectabile, Aster, Camellia, Chrysanthemum.*

Lunar Symbolism
In Bronze Age Cyprus (c.2500–1050 BCE) moon symbolism was incorporated into religious practices, although it's difficult to identify with certainty, excavations at Enkomi uncovered female figurines with crescent-shaped headdresses dating to approximately 1600–1050 BCE. Terracotta figurines dating to the late Bronze Age display celestial imagery, including what some scholars interpret as lunar symbols were found at the sanctuary of Ayia Irini.

The main goddess was referred to as Wanassa (the Queen of the Heavens) and incorporated lunar aspects within her broader divine role. The work of Dr Karageorghis reveals the history of the great goddess of Cyprus, who was later syncretized with various goddesses including Aphrodite, and who appears to have maintained lunar associations throughout her complex evolution. Archaeological evidence from the sanctuary at Paphos, traditionally associated with this goddess, has yielded artifacts with lunar symbolism, including crescent-shaped pendants and disc-shaped ornaments dating from the Late Bronze Age through the Archaic period. During the Hellenistic period (323–30 BCE), Cypriot religion became increasingly syncretized with Greek traditions, and lunar worship became more explicitly associated with specific deities. Inscriptional evidence from Salamis references worship of Artemis Selene, directly combining the Greek goddess Artemis with her lunar aspect. An important find is an inscription from Kourion dating to the 1st century BCE that mentions a priestess of Artemis Phosphoros (Light-bringer), for which we have already seen this epithet used to describe Hekate and the association between Hekate and Artemis. There is some evidence that Cypriot sanctuaries were designed with lunar observations in mind. The sanctuary of Aphrodite at Palaepaphos, for example, has architectural features that some scholars interpret as facilitating lunar observations for ritual purposes. A 3rd century BCE inscription from Kafizin mentions offerings made during the full moon, suggesting ritual timing based on lunar phases.

Evidence for specifically Cypriot moon-based calendar systems is fragmentary, but there are indications that lunar months were observed for religious purposes. An inscription from Salamis dating to the Hellenistic period references a festival held in the month of Artemisios at the full moon. Epigraphic evidence from the Hellenistic period suggests that Cyprus generally followed the lunar calendar common throughout the Greek world, with local variations. Months with names like Artemisios (associated with Artemis/moon) and Selenios (directly named after the moon) appear in Cypriot inscriptions.

There is also evidence of a festival called Karpeia, which is associated with the full moon occurring during harvest time (typically autumn). This suggests that agricultural cycles were integrated with lunar observations. An inscription from Paphos mentions ceremonies conducted during the winter full moon, suggesting that the midwinter full moon held special significance in Cypriot religious practice. There is also evidence from Amathus indicating that the spring full moon was associated with rituals for young women, possibly related to fertility and marriage. The term Parthenos Selene (Maiden Moon) appears in a fragmentary inscription dating to the 1st century BCE.

British Lunar Traditions

British lunar traditions originally derive from a Germanic calendar that had been brought to England from mainland Europe by Anglo-Saxon settlers, and was used to divide the year into 12, or sometimes 13 lunar months. The earliest and most detailed account available of this calendar comes from St. Bede, an 8th century monk and scholar based in Jarrow in northeast England, who outlined the old Anglo-Saxon months of the year in his work *De temporum ratione* (The Reckoning of Time), in AD 725.

Bede was working with corresponding Anglo-Saxon names and explained that what is now January corresponds to an Anglo-Saxon month known as Æftera Geola, or After Yule, which is generally accepted to be based on the Norse festival of Jol. This was associated with the winter solstice, and a time when spirits of the dead passed to the otherworld and were honoured and celebrated. February (Sōlmōnath) is possibly derived from an old English word for wet sand or mud, (sōl). According to Bede, it was the month of cakes, when ritual offerings of savoury cakes and loaves of bread would be made to ensure a good year's harvest. The connection between old English mud and Bede's "month of cakes" continues to be debated with some suggesting that Bede made a mistake.

It's also suggested that the name Sōlmōnath might have referred to the cakes' sandy, gritty texture. March was Hrēðmonath to the Anglo-Saxons, and was named in honour of a fertility goddess, Hreða, or Rheda. Her name eventually became Lide in some southern dialects of English, and the name Lide or Lide-month continued in parts of southwest England until as recently as the 19th century. April corresponds to the Anglo-Saxon Eostremonath, which according to Bede, took its name from the goddess Eostre. She is thought to have been a goddess of the dawn who was honoured with a festival around the time of the spring equinox, which, according to some accounts, eventually morphed into Easter. This, however, is debated as there is little existing evidence of veneration of the Goddess Eostre. May (Thrimilce) was the month of three milkings, when livestock were often so well fed on fresh spring grass that they could be milked three times a day. June and July were together known as Liða, an old English word meaning mild or gentle, which referred to the period of warm, seasonable weather either side of Midsummer. To differentiate between the two, June was sometimes known as Ærraliða, or 'before-mild', and July was Æfteraliða, or 'after-mild'. In some years a 'leap month' was added to the calendar at the height of the summer, which was Thriliða, or the 'third-mild'. August (Weodmonat) or the 'plant month'.

After that came September, (Hāligmonath), meaning 'holy month', when celebrations and religious festivals would be held to celebrate a successful summer's crop. October (Winterfylleth), or the 'winter full moon', because, as Bede explained, winter was said to begin on the first full moon in October. November (Blōtmonath) was 'the month of blood sacrifices'. No one is quite sure what the purpose of this late autumnal sacrifice would have been, but it's likely that any older or infirm livestock that seemed unlikely to see out bad weather ahead would be killed both as a stockpile of food, and as an offering for a safe and mild winter. December, (Ærra Geola) or the month before Yule, after which Æftera Geola would come round again.

Modern English names for the months go back to Roman times. For example, January is from Janus, the name of the Roman god of entrances and gateways, (sound vaguely familiar?) Like Hekate, Janus is said to be perpetually both looking backward into the year that had just passed and forward into the year that is to come.

February takes its name from Februa, which was a Roman festival of purification and cleanliness, and March is named after Mars, the Roman god of war. April is believed to be related to the Latin verb aperire, which means 'to open,' and is assumed to reflect the opening of spring flowers. May and June both venerate two goddesses Maia and Juno. July and August assume their names from Julius and Augustus Caesar. September, October, November and December were originally the seventh (septem), eighth (octo), ninth (novem), and tenth (decem) months of the Roman calendar.

Using some of these old names and associations I undertook further research to acquire white-flowering and moon-related magickal and medicinal plants. I began to identify the plants associated with the moon.

The poppy appears in Cypriot moon veneration — terracotta figurines from the sanctuary of Ayia Irini depict goddesses holding what appear to be poppy capsules — so I introduced white poppies. Also from Cypriot traditions, I included *Artemisia vulgaris* (mugwort) and *Artemisia absinthium*, which was used in Cypriot ritual contexts, particularly in purification ceremonies associated with lunar cycles. However, I wanted to ensure that botanicals associated with Hekate were central in my planting choices, so my selections included several different perspectives. Alongside the obvious parameters of space and suitable climate, I considered the aromatic properties of the plants associated with Hekate, such as storax, frankincense, myrrh, sage and cypress, which produce strong, distinctive aromas when burned or crushed. This reflects the importance of fumigation in creating an appropriate atmosphere for divine communication, and the belief that certain scents could attract or repel specific spiritual entities. Also, there is the psychoactive potential that exists in mandrake, nightshade, and wormwood, all of which contain compounds capable of altering consciousness, reflecting Hekate's association with visionary experiences and transitions between different states of awareness.

The third aspect was the chthonic connections relating to Hekate's links to death, the underworld, or transitions, such as cypress trees in cemeteries, yew's funerary associations, and garlic's dual role as both offering and protection. Finally, liminal habitats; several plants associated with Hekate naturally grow in boundary spaces, including pennyroyal near water margins, nightshade in the transitions between cultivated and wild spaces, and wormwood along roadsides and paths. The following, is a list of the main plants in my moon garden. Since completing the moon garden, I have begun work on my 'dark moon' garden which is a space to celebrate the darker side of botanicals, and is where I have relocated my poisonous plants, and planted black and dark-coloured flowers.

Plants in the Full Moon Garden
Instead of an alphabetic ordering of the plants, I have described them by each bed. In the first bed there are roses, wisteria, a Japanese anemone, a viburnum and white poppies.

Rose: Maintains eye health, healthy hair and skin. Lowers blood pressure, eliminates acne and bad breath, aids relaxation and treats menstrual pain. Place around sprains and dark bruises to help them heal faster. Used in love spells and rituals to attract love and enhance feelings of passion and romance. Roses have the power to heal emotional wounds and promote self-love. They are often included in Hekatean magic.
Planet: Venus
Element: Water
Deities: Demeter, Isis, Eros, Cupid and Hathor

Wisteria: Is an antioxidant with antibacterial properties. Its flowers are edible whilst the stems are poisonous. Wisteria is associated with Mercury and the element of Air. Its most common magical associations include psychic development, wisdom and meditation.

Dinner Plate Dahlia: Reduce glucose levels by producing insulin (tubers). Used for spells associated with dignity.

Anemone: Its immunomodulatory, anti-inflammatory, antioxidant and antimicrobial qualities were used in amulets for protection against sorcery. In Germany the anemone was known as 'hexenblumen', (witches' flower.) In England, picking the flowers was said to bring on thunderstorms.
Planet: Mars
Element: Fire
Deities: Adonis Aphrodite

Viburnum Opulus: Also known as cramp bark, it is used as a skeletal and muscle relaxant. Cramp Bark helps to circulate energy and alleviate congestion. It is also used in spells to enhance emotional healing, love and compassion. The berries are poisonous, although are considered edible after cooking.
Planets: Venus, Saturn, Neptune
Moon phase: Waxing Moon

Paperverum Rhoes: A good astringent, used to treat diarrhoea and dysentery. Aids sleep, and attracts love, luck, fertility and money when carried or consumed. Poppy seeds make particularly good offerings to the dead.
Planet: Moon
Element: water
Deities: Demeter Hypnos

In the second bed there are geraniums, cerastium, jasmine, hibiscus, hostas, abelia, sedum and Gaura.

Geranium macrorrhizum: Relieves stress, alleviates pain due to wounds and is used for premenstrual problems, nausea, diarrhoea and gall stones. White geranium promotes fertility, red geranium for health and warning of visitors.
Planet: Venus
Element: water

Cerastium tomentosum: Is often used as a ground cover plant. It has anti-inflammatory, antimicrobial, and antioxidant properties. It is used in treating digestive and respiratory ailments. The leaves have a slightly bitter and slightly sweet taste.

Jasmine: Has been used for liver disease (hepatitis), pain due to liver scarring (cirrhosis), and abdominal pain due to severe diarrhoea (dysentery). It is also used to prevent strokes, for relaxation (as a sedative), to heighten sexual desire (as an aphrodisiac), and in cancer treatment. It promotes spiritual awakening and is used in love spells.
Planet: Moon
Element: Water
Deities: Vishnu

Hibiscus: Has antiseptic properties, antispasmodic properties (blood pressure-lowering properties, a mild laxative effect, diuretic effect (increases urine production) and has antioxidant properties. With its historical use as an aphrodisiac, hibiscus carries potent energies associated with love and lust, making it a staple ingredient in love spells and rituals.
Planet: Venus
Element: Water

Hosta: Anti-inflammatory and analgesic effects. Peace and resilience.

Abelia: Attracts butterflies, symbolizes growth, prosperity, and nature's connection.

Sedum Spectabile: Treats coughs, high blood pressure and wound healing. Used in spells to enhance peace, perseverance, and calmness.

Gaura: A decoction of the roots is used to treat snakebites (Hopi), and as a burn dressing and to treat inflammation (Navajo). It symbolises purity, spirituality, and enlightenment.

In the third bed there are Saccoccia, echinacea, asters, a philadelphus and agapanthus:

Saccoccia: Treats stomach pain, rheumatism, sore throats and traumatic injuries. (Traditional Chinese Medicine).

Echinacea: Shortens the duration of the common cold and flu, and reduces symptoms such as sore throats (pharyngitis), coughs and fevers. Used in spells for prosperity and defence/protection spells.

Aster: Treatment of weak skin, pain, fevers and diarrhoea. Ancient Greeks used asters to ward off evil spirits and would burn them as a way to repel serpents from their homes. They would also weave asters into wreaths and place them on altars to honour Hekate.
Planet: Venus.
Element: Water.
Deities: Venus

Philadelphus: A poultice of the bruised leaves has been used to treat infected breasts. A strained decoction of the branches, sometimes with the flowers, has been used as a soaking solution in the treatment of sore chests. Used in the treatment of eczema and bleeding haemorrhoids. Promotes healing and tranquillity.

Agapanthus: Treats heart disease, paralysis, coughs, colds and other ailments, and the leaves are used as bandages (the plant contains anti-inflammatory chemicals. Also used as an aphrodisiac in some African traditions, (Xhosa), and may also be used as a fertility charm and carried by pregnant women to protect and ensure the health of an unborn child.

The fourth bed contains hellebores, lilies, peonies, a honeysuckle and an old grapevine that was in place before I began planting.

Helleborus Natale: Used to treat cholera, gout and high blood pressure. Used in rituals to repel evil. Scattering before you renders you invisible. Astral projection exorcisms.
Planet: Saturn
Element: Water

Lilium muscat: Treats severe anxiety. Lilies are associated with the moon, water, and emotions. Protection to repel baneful magick, negative energies and spirits/entities. Protects property and those within it. Used to repel love or, to grow and attract love. Use in spells and rituals to bring strength, peace, and harmony.
Planet: Moon.
Element: Water.
Deities: Venus and Juno

Peony: Inflammation, pain, and liver diseases. Peony is named after Paeon, a healing deity who healed Hades' and Ares' wounds. Paeon was a student of Asclepius. Protection, and exorcism.
Planet: Sun.
Element: Fire

Honeysuckle: To promote sweating, as a laxative, to counteract poisoning and for birth control. To attract friends, bring in luck, and sustain love in the home where it grows. Honeysuckle is especially liked by fairies. Psychic protection.
Planet: Jupiter.
Element: Earth

Fragalosa grape vine: Treats diabetes, high cholesterol, high blood pressure, osteoarthritis. Grape leaves are used as an ingredient in a spell to bring abundance. For a simple talisman, fold a grape leaf around a silver coin, and tie with green string. Carry this in your pocket to bring you prosperity.

In the fifth bed there are foxgloves, aconite, hydrangea, a camelia, wormwood and mugwort

Foxglove: Treats congestive heart failure and heart rhythm problems.
Faeries were often depicted with a foxglove bell for a hat. The foxglove is used to lure faeries and was believed to be effective in breaking their enchantment over humans. Protection used to make black dye and paint on thresholds.
Planet: Venus.
Element: Water

Camelia: Reduces the enlargement of the heart, improves blood pressure dysfunction, and restores antioxidant enzyme activity. The camellia brings riches and luxury and so is used in spells of this kind. Place the fresh blossoms in vessels of water on the altar during money and prosperity rituals.
Planet: Moon.
Element: Water

Aconite: Treats anxiety, and restlessness, acute sudden fever, symptoms from exposure to dry, cold weather or very hot weather, tingling, coldness and numbness, influenza or colds with congestion; and heavy, pulsating headaches. Protection from evil. It has a history of being used for protection from malevolent spirits and negative energies.

Hydrangea: Treats bladder infections, prostate infections, enlarged prostates, kidney stones and other conditions. In China, hydrangeas are associated with heartfelt apologies and are known as 'the flowers of the Eight Immortals'.

The Eight Immortals are legendary figures revered in Taoism. In one tale, the forces of the Immortals and the Dragon King clash. To apologize, the Dragon King offers seven of the Immortals beautiful hydrangea flowers.

Wormwood: Reduces pain and swelling, treats digestion problems, intestinal worms, and skin infections. Associated with psychic abilities and divination, making it a key ingredient in rituals and spells. According to legend, burning wormwood in a graveyard is thought to evoke the spirits of the departed. Wormwood's ability to evoke spirits makes it a particularly useful witchcraft herb during Samhain.

Mugwort: Treats digestive problems, irregular menstruation and high blood pressure. Named after the luna goddess Artemis. Used in smudge sticks for cleansing spaces, and in dream pillows.

In the sixth bed there is a cherry tree. In fact, there are actually two. The first is the winter flowering cherry I bought, and the second is a spring flowering cherry which somehow arrived of its own accord. There are also white periwinkles, white strawberry plants and miniature white roses.

Winter-flowering Cherry: Is a rejuvenating tonic and aphrodisiac but also a mild, sleep-enhancing remedy.

White Periwinkle: Is said to treat leukaemia, Hodgkin disease, malignant lymphomas, neuroblastoma, Wilms tumour, Kaposi sarcoma, mycosis fungoides.

It improves cerebral blood flow and treats high blood pressure. It protects against evil, baneful spirits, snakes, poison, wild beasts and terror. The dried leaves are good for smudging to clear away negative energy. Periwinkle is also associated with memory; specifically, gazing at a periwinkle flower is said to bring back lost memories.

White Strawberry: The antioxidant compounds found in strawberries protect cells and tissue in the body by neutralizing free radicals. Attracts success, good fortune and favourable circumstances. Served as a love food. Leaves are carried for luck. Pregnant women carry a packet of the leaves to ease the pain of pregnancy.

White Miniature Rose: Lowers blood pressure, eliminates acne, aids relaxation, eliminates bad breath and treats menstrual pain. Place around sprains and dark bruises to help them heal faster. Wild roses are also associated with spiritual transformation and healing.

There are many botanicals are associated with Hekate. Some are associated with votive offering such as during the Deipnon, such as garlic. Other plants are used in rituals such as a 13-leaf branch of laurel. Others (such as aconite) are used in spell casting.

Some have a more oracular use in divination or dream work, and others for their psychoactive properties and inducing trans-like states. There are also botanicals used symbolically, representing Hekate's capacity in transversing between worlds or reflecting some of the lunar aspects and energies. Here are some of the most important botanicals that relate to Hekate. They are not all in my moon or dark moon gardens, but most are easy to collect if not grow.

The herbal associations were documented in several sources. For example, Theophrastus in *Historia Plantarum* mentions garlic (specifically black garlic), which is used in purification before rituals, while Rue is hung at crossroads during the Deipnon, and aconite and dittany of Crete are used in fumigation. Black poppies are also used in offerings.

The Strophalos
As with many gardens, there are not only plants, but other things. In my moon garden there is also an altar space, cauldrons, ornaments, statues, crystals and all manner of other things associated with the moon and Hekate. At the end of the moon garden there is an old winch that was originally used to draw water from a well.

It has been there for many years, and I had never really paid much attention to it until I started building the moon garden and realised it is something that I think is important, at least to me. The Strophalos (στρόφαλος) is one of the key signatures of Hekate. It is often described as a 'witch's wheel', and as such has been adopted by Wiccans and modern pagans as a magical symbol associated with the 'meandering of the mind'.

I have never been convinced of this view of Hekate's Strophalos, or that it is actually a wheel. There is a growing body of thought acknowledging that the symbol most often associated with the concept of Hekate's Wheel is a relatively modern invention of unknown origin. This leaves us with the mystery of what Hekate's Strophalos actually was, and how it was used.

The Strophalos has often been confused with the Iynx. However, it is my contention that they are two completely different tools. The most common description of the Iynx is as a physical tool used in love magic. It consisted of a small wheel or disc and was often made of bronze or wood and attached to strings that would be stretched between the fingers. When the wheel was spun, it created a whirring noise that had magical properties. The term derives from the wryneck bird (*Jynx torquilla*).

The Greek name was iunx, whose distinctive neck-twisting movements may have inspired the rotating motion of the magical wheel. The iunx bird was also connected with magical practices, including divination and love spells and is understood to be the root to the work 'jinx'.

Archaeological evidence has confirmed the existence of iynges (plural of iynx). Several bronze wheels that match the description of the iynx have been discovered at various sites in Greece, they are typically small (about one to three inches in diameter) with holes for attaching strings. The iynx appears in the Second Idyll of Theocritus, called *The Sorceress*, where the protagonist Simaetha uses it in a love spell: 'Turn, magic wheel, draw homeward him I love.' Pindar describes the iynx as a tool first given by Aphrodite to Jason to help him win Medea's love.

In the PGM, the lynx appears in several contexts. The term is sometimes used metaphorically to refer to compelling forces or as a technical term for certain types of spells. There is a 'spell of attraction' that includes instructions similar to traditional lynx use, though the word itself isn't always used explicitly. The papyri sometimes describe the lynx in connection with celestial powers, suggesting its use in astral magic, and contain references to the 'cosmic iynx', suggesting an expanded meaning beyond the simple love charm.

Whilst archaeological evidence has confirmed the existence of iynges, to date there is no archaeological evidence that can show what the Strophalos looks like. So, to achieve a better understanding, it is necessary to turn to descriptions from ancient sources and the etymology of the word.

One of the most significant ancient references to the Strophalos appears in fragmentary remains of the *Chaldean Oracles*. Fragment 26 specifically mentions the Strophalos of Hekate. Michael Psellos when commenting on the Chaldean Oracles described the Strophalos as 'a golden sphere enclosing a lapis lazuli. It has a leather thong for swinging it round and round. It is everywhere marked with characters. Whirl this and utter cries...'

This description provides several details about the physical form of this magical tool as a golden spherical container, enclosing lapis lazuli, that is attached to a leather strap for rotation and is inscribed with magical characters or symbols and used in conjunction with ritual vocalisations.

The *Chaldean Oracle* context suggests its use in theurgical rites, most likely as part of rituals designed to invoke or communicate with Hekate. Within the Neoplatonic interpretations of the Chaldean system, the Strophalos takes on significant cosmic symbolism. According to these interpretations, the motion of the Strophalos represents the cosmic revolutions of celestial bodies, and the circular movement of divine energy or power and possibly the soul's journey between cosmic realms. It has been argued that the Strophalos, through its circular motion, was thought to somehow mimic the circular motion of the cosmos and thereby facilitate contact with divine forces. With this interpretation, the lapis lazuli could symbolise the celestial realm, while the golden sphere could represent solar principles or divine perfection with inscriptions, possibly as 'voces magicae' or incantations, or symbols establishing connections with specific cosmic powers.

Etymologically, the term Strophalos derives from the Greek root στρέφω (strephō), meaning 'to turn' or 'to twist'. A literal translation of the Greek word Strophalos is winch. It is not used to describe free-spinning wheels. The Greek word for wheel is ρόδα (roda) or τροχός (which refers more to a grindstone). So, if Hekate's Strophalos was actually a wheel, it would have been more appropriately named Hekate's Roda or Trochós. As it isn't we assume that it was never a wheel.

There are several archaic references to rotating devices used in rituals, and the descriptions often emphasise the controlled nature of the motion, suggesting mechanisms more complex than simple wheels. This suggests a device that needed to maintain specific orientations during use something more easily achieved with a winch mechanism than a free- spinning wheel.

Moreover, the practical aspects of theurgic ritual as described in late antique sources suggest that the Strophalos was used to manipulate something tangible — perhaps ritual cords or other materials. This functional requirement aligns better with a winch mechanism than a symbolic wheel. The argument gains further support when we consider the broader context of Greco-Roman mechanical technology.

By the Hellenistic period, sophisticated winch mechanisms were widely used in both secular and religious contexts. The temple machinery described by Vitruvius in *De Architectura* shows that complex mechanical devices were not unusual in religious settings.

The word στροφεύς (stropheus), from the same root, refers specifically to a type of socket-hinge mechanism.

According to Michael Psellos, the Strophalos was 'animated with tireless motion'. The key here is that this motion is described as controlled and purposeful, more consistent with a winch mechanism than a simple wheel. There is archaeological evidence of contemporary mechanical devices. Greek and Roman winch mechanisms, particularly those used in temples, showing a sophisticated understanding of controlled rotational forces. The mechanics described by Hero of Alexandria in his *Mechanica* demonstrate that such devices were well-understood and commonly used in religious contexts. The ritual context provides further evidence in that the Strophalos was described as an instrument for drawing down (κατάγω) divine powers. This specific terminology of 'drawing down' suggests a vertical motion more consistent with a winch than a wheel. In practical terms, a winch mechanism would provide the controlled, steady motion necessary for ritual purposes, whereas a simple wheel would lack this precise control. For me, it becomes clear that the Strophalos is not a wheel but a winch, and was used to draw down, or maybe, if we take into consideration Hekate's chthonic role, to draw up, and was most likely used in the more theurgic practices.

Coming back to my own story, when I was driven to create my moon garden, I tried many spaces before being called to place it directly in front of the house, in a space where we found a key and that already housed an old winch. As a part of the consecration of my moon garden, I adorned the Strophalos with serpent heads.

The serpentine imagery associated with Hekate evolved significantly over time. In archaic and classical Greek periods (7th–4th centuries BCE), explicit serpent iconography appears limited, with Hekate more commonly depicted as a beautiful, torch-bearing maiden. During the Hellenistic period (3rd–1st centuries BCE), as Hekate's chthonic aspects gained prominence, serpent imagery became more common, particularly in magical contexts. By the Roman Imperial period (1st–4th centuries CE), serpents had become standard attributes in Hekate's iconography, appearing in statuary, reliefs, and magical artefacts across the Mediterranean world. In late antiquity, Neoplatonic philosophers and theurgists elaborated on the symbolic significance of Hekate's serpents, interpreting them as representations of cosmic forces and divine energies.

The snakes reflect Hekate's serpentine connections and appear to derive from several traditions. Serpents featured prominently in Greek magical traditions, particularly those involving chthonic deities.

The PGM contains numerous spells invoking Hekate that include serpent imagery or actual use of snake parts, suggesting a practical magical tradition that reinforced the association. In addition, serpents are associated with healing and Hekate maintained aspects relating to plant knowledge and healing, which is one of the primary functions of the moon garden. This  connection may have strengthened the serpentine symbolism, particularly in her role as a goddess of herbal knowledge. As a goddess with strong connections to the underworld, crossroads, and liminal spaces, Hekate naturally affiliated with creatures perceived to dwell close to or beneath the earth. Serpents, moving directly against the ground and often living in burrows, embodied this chthonic quality. Finally, Hekate's association with snakes may derive from syncretism with Anatolian goddesses, particularly Cybele and Kubaba, who were often depicted with serpents as symbols of fertility and regeneration.

At the Temple of Artemis in Ephesus, several statuettes dating from the 4th–3rd centuries BCE depict Hekate with serpents entwined around her arms or at her feet. These representations emphasise her role as Potnia Theron (mistress of animals), which was an epithet also given to Artemis, Persephone and others with specific dominion over wild animals. Another artefact is a second century CE marble relief from Pergamon showing triple-formed Hekate with serpents emerging from her shoulders, clearly establishing the serpent as an integral aspect of her physical manifestation.

There are also several Roman artefacts that depict Hekate holding torches and whips with serpents at her feet or emerging from her hair. These were often used for protective or binding magic and demonstrate the continued importance of the serpentine imagery in practical magical applications. There are also bronze figurines from various sites in Asia Minor that show Hekate with snake-entwined torches or holding serpents directly, and clay votive tablets in the sanctuary of Demeter and Persephone at Eleusis that occasionally depict Hekate with serpentine attributes, connecting her chthonic aspects with Eleusinian mystery traditions.

The serpent carries multiple symbolic meanings in relation to Hekate, it represents transformation and renewal, reflected in the snake's ability to shed its skin, which made it a powerful symbol of rebirth and transformation, aligning with Hekate's role in transitions and liminal spaces. In her chthonic nature, serpents represented Hekate's connection to the underworld and hidden wisdom. Their ability to move between visible and hidden realms paralleled Hekate's own liminal nature. In many contexts, serpents served protective functions against evil. Hekate's serpents symbolised her ability to guard against malevolent forces, particularly at vulnerable thresholds like doorways and crossroads. Serpents also carry associations with feminine power, fertility, and the mysteries of birth and death. These aspects aligned with Hekate's character as a powerful female deity operating outside normal social constraints. Finally, serpents are often connected with hidden knowledge and prophetic powers, complementing Hekate's associations with magic and mysteries.

The Dark Moon Garden
It is interesting that Hekate's explicit lunar associations developed gradually, becoming more pronounced during the Classical and Hellenistic periods. By the time of the composition of the *Homeric Hymn to Demeter*,

Hekate is portrayed carrying torches to illuminate the darkness; a characteristic that would later connect her to the illuminating quality of the moon.

Hekate's association with the dark moon represents her most profound and enduring lunar connection, representing a liminal period and the transition between lunar cycles, making it a natural celestial embodiment of Hekate's domain. The dark moon, as a time of transition that perfectly symbolises Hekate's essential nature as a goddess of passages and transformation.

The dark moon refers to the period when the moon is not visible in the night sky, which encompasses more than just the astronomical moment of the new moon. Astronomically speaking, this is the waning crescent phase immediately before the new moon. The day or so after the astronomical calculation of new moon, the crescent mostly remains too thin to be visible to the naked eye. Many ancient lunar calendars, including early Greek and Babylonian systems, began the month not with the astronomical new moon, but with the first visible crescent after the dark moon period. This distinction was practical rather than theoretical for civilisations lacking astronomical instruments. The first visible crescent provided a reliable observable marker for calendar-keeping, while the astronomical new moon remained invisible, and its exact timing could only be estimated or calculated rather than directly observed. Many of the rituals associated with Hekate are determined under particular phases of the moon, and some of the most significant in the dark moon phase. Contemporary pagan, Wiccan and other spiritual practices often maintain a clear distinction between dark moon and new moon rituals. These traditions often associate the dark moon with completion, banishing, introspection and deep meditation, while the new moon relates to beginnings, setting intentions and initiating projects.

My first Moon Garden clearly reflected the new beginnings and growth aspect, but I also wanted to celebrate the more chthonic aspects of Hekate. I decided to create a new space that reflected this, and the dark moon that is associated with death and the underworld as the absence of the moon from the sky symbolising a journey to the unseen realm.

Hekate's role as psychopomp and her connections to the underworld makes the dark moon an appropriate celestial manifestation of her power. It is in this expression of her role as a mediator between worlds that we can understand and appreciate the significance of the association of the dark moon.

There is some archaeological evidence for this connection, from curse tablets invoking Hekate, which were often buried during the dark moon phase. Several specimens recovered from the Athenian Agora and other sites specifically reference the dark moon in their invocations to Hekate. Ancient magical papyri and literary sources indicate that rituals invoking Hekate were often performed during the dark moon phase.

The Greek Magical Papyri contain numerous invocations to Hekate specifically timed to the dark moon. For example, a ritual to Hekate to be performed 'when the moon is invisible'.

Theocritus' *Idyll 2,* known as The Sorceress, portrays a woman performing magic with invocations to Hekate during a moonless night, further demonstrating this connection in popular understanding.

Hekate's identification with a triad of lunar goddesses was often visualised as a triple-formed deity representing the three phases of the moon. In this conception, Hekate was frequently syncretised with Artemis, representing the waxing moon or maiden aspect and Selene representing the full moon or mother aspect, while Hekate herself primarily represented the waning or dark moon, which is considered the crone aspect.

This triple goddess association is visually represented in numerous artefacts from the period, including the Hekataion pillars showing three connected female figures. During the Roman period, further syncretism occurred as Hekate became increasingly identified directly with Selene (Luna in Roman terminology), the goddess embodying the full moon itself. This amalgamation is evident in Apuleius' *Metamorphoses,* which is also known as *The Golden Ass,* where the goddess Isis describes herself as manifesting in multiple forms including 'three-formed Hecate' and 'Selene, the moon'. As a consequence of Hekate's evolution as a lunar goddess, magical operations and chthonic rituals typically invoke her dark moon aspect, while purification rituals and more public worship connects to her full moon associations.

The dual association might also reflect a spiritual notion of cosmic completeness, with Hekate embodying both extremes of lunar manifestations: the total darkness and full illumination reflecting her comprehensive power. In embodying both ends of lunar cycle, Hekate demonstrates her complete command over this celestial domain.

So, the dark moon garden was conceived as a space to celebrate Hekate's dark moon associations, and encompass a darker side of magic, poisons and potions. It's interesting that in old hospital and convent gardens it is possible to find many of what today would be considered deadly poisons. As the opposite of my first moon garden, the dark moon garden is designed to be filled with poisonous plants and dark flowers. The structural starting point was a metal pergola, that immediately gave it a gothic feel, I wanted to create a space that felt forbidding, lost and slightly abandoned. This initial planting plan contained Black Baccara roses, Queen of the Night tulips, *Atropa belladonna*, black henbane, black hellebores, Digitalis, *Datura stramonium* (witch's' thornapple) *Agapanthus africanus* 'Black Magic', Aconite. In the centre I placed some ceramic tiles; they are not fixed or complete and add to the sense of a place lost in time. There is ivy climbing the pergola, and new planting of a dark buddleia and more black tulips. The dark moon garden is far from complete and proving a greater challenge than the much bigger original Moon Garden, but then, I expected it would. The research and creation of the dark moon garden led to greater research and interest in dark botanicals and what is inside the witches garden and cupboards, this has become the basis for a number of podcasts, articles and workshops on the topic.

As I mentioned in my introduction, even today, green magic is often perceived as the more 'folksy' and a more basic form of magickal practice. It's certainly less sexy than the more serious ceremonial and theurgic practices, yet the power to kill or cure is there at your fingertips. Centuries of potion makers and poisoners begin at the same point, with their hands in the soil, tending and growing a multitude of botanicals. Here are some examples of the kill and cure potential of some of the most well-known dark botanicals.

Aconite (*Aconitum napellus*): Known as monkshood, wolf's bane and devil's helmet, aconite stands as perhaps the most infamous member of the witch's pharmacopoeia. Its blue-hooded flowers belie its deadly nature, for aconite contains aconitine, among the most potent naturally occurring cardiac poisons known. In the hands of the skilled herbalist, aconite served as a powerful analgesic.

Medieval texts, including the work of Hildegard von Bingen (12th century), document its application as an external unguent for neuralgia and rheumatic conditions. The Salernitan herbal tradition, from the Salerno medica school, prescribed extraordinarily dilute preparations (typically one part plant material to 10,000 parts water or oil) for the treatment of fevers and inflammation.

In some Alpine communities, wisewomen prepared a salve of aconite root (approximately the size of a small pea, never more) macerated in goose fat, applied externally to relieve the pain of gout. The dosage was critical; the preparation would never contain more than 0.5 grams of dried root per 30 grams of fat. Aconite's association with the underworld made it central to numerous magical practices. The 16th-century grimoire *Le Petit Albert* includes a formula for shape-shifting ointment with aconite as a primary ingredient.

It was believed that the plant's ability to induce a sensation of flying stemmed from its influence over the boundary between worlds.

In a dark moon ritual from Carinthia, Austria, practitioners would place a minute amount of powdered aconite root (less than 0.1 gram) beneath their tongue whilst performing divination rituals. The resulting numbness and altered sensation were interpreted as signs of connection with ancestral spirits. As a poison, aconite's efficiency is legendary. Historical accounts suggest that as little as 2–6 milligrams of purified aconitine could prove fatal. The plant earned its epithet 'wolf's bane' from its historical use in poisoned baits set for predators. The symptoms of aconite poisoning are particularly gruesome, beginning with tingling and numbness of the mouth and extremities, progressing to vomiting and diarrhoea, then paralysis of the respiratory system whilst the victim remains conscious until the final moments. Medieval court records from the trial of Catherine La Voisin, a notorious poisoner in the court of Louis XIV, reveal the use of aconite distillations so potent that three drops in wine would cause death within hours. The victim would appear to have succumbed to natural causes, specifically, heart failure making detection nearly impossible given the medical knowledge of the era.

Black Henbane (*Hyoscyamus niger*): With its sticky foliage and bell-shaped, veined flowers of dingy yellow, black henbane presents a somewhat unassuming look. Yet within its tissues lie hyoscyamine and scopolamine, tropane alkaloids capable of profound effects upon body and mind. Henbane's sedative and antispasmodic properties made it invaluable to medieval medicine. The *Lacnunga,* an Anglo-Saxon medical text, describes a sleep-inducing tonic prepared from approximately 1 gram of Henbane seed steeped in wine. For the treatment of toothache, practitioners would place a small quantity (typically 0.25 grams) of crushed seed upon the affected tooth, providing relief through localised anaesthesia. The herbalist Nicholas Culpeper recommended henbane oil (made by infusing 30 grams of crushed seed in 500 millilitres of olive oil) as a treatment for inflamed joints and 'nervous agitations'. The preparation would be applied externally only, never ingested. Henbane features prominently in Scandinavian magical tradition, where it was known as Bilsa or Bolmört. There are examples to its inclusion in seiðr practices — Norse shamanic rituals seeking prophetic visions. The plant was burned as an incense (approximately 0.5 grams of dried leaf) during ceremonies to invoke Hel, goddess of the underworld.

The 17th-century *Compendium Maleficarum* describes confessions (albeit extracted under torture) of witches who incorporated henbane into flying ointments. The resulting hallucinations, particularly the sensation of flight, would have been consistent with the plant's anticholinergic effects. Magical protection spells often called for henbane to be planted at the four corners of a dwelling, as its association with Saturn was believed to ward off malevolent spirits and the evil eye.

Though less immediately deadly than aconite, henbane remains profoundly dangerous. Ingestion of 10–15 grams of plant material could prove fatal, preceded by hallucinations, extreme thirst, and cardiac arrhythmia. Death results from respiratory failure, often after a period of delirium so extreme that victims might harm themselves inadvertently during hallucinatory episodes.

The Scottish *Chronicle of Fife* records a particularly disturbing incident from 1393 in which monks at a monastery accidentally consumed ale brewed with henbane instead of hops. While none died, the entire brotherhood suffered profound hallucinations for several days, with some reportedly unable to recognise their own identities for weeks afterward.

Atropa Belladonna (Deadly Nightshade): Perhaps no plant better embodies the duality of healing and harm than *belladonna*, with its glossy black berries and solitary purple-brown flowers. Named for Atropos, the Fate who cuts the thread of life, *belladonna* contains atropine and scopolamine in concentrations sufficient to both heal and destroy.

Renaissance physicians valued *belladonna* extracts for their ability to relax smooth muscle and dilate the pupils. Women would place a single drop of highly diluted *belladonna* extract (approximately 1 part plant juice to 100 parts water) in their eyes to dilate the pupils — a practice that gave the plant its common name, 'bella donna' meaning 'beautiful lady' in Italian.

Less lovely is the treatment of intestinal spasms, where practitioners would administer minuscule doses, typically tinctures containing the equivalent of 0.05–0.1 grams of leaf material to relieve pain and cramping.

The 16th-century physician Paracelsus reportedly prescribed *belladonna* preparations (in quantities less than 0.3 grams of leaf) for the treatment of Parkinson's-like tremors. Belladonna's association with Hekate made it central to divination rituals throughout Europe. There are examples from the Romanian Carpathians where practitioners would consume a barely perceptible amount of *belladonna* berry juice (less than 0.1 millilitres) before scrying in dark mirrors or still water. The resulting pupil dilation would allow maximum light gathering in dim conditions, whilst the mild hallucinogenic effects were believed to open the inner eye.

In Baltic witch traditions, there is a ritual involving the placement of *belladonna* leaves beneath the pillow (never more than three leaves) to induce prophetic dreams. Similarly, Renaissance grimoires describe the use of *belladonna* as an ingredient in summoning rituals, particularly those aimed at manifesting lunar deities.

The deadly nature of *belladonna* cannot be overstated; ingestion of 10–20 berries would prove fatal to an adult. Death comes through anti-cholinergic poisoning, manifesting as hyperthermia, confusion, hallucinations, tachycardia and ultimately respiratory collapse. Court records from 16th-century Venice document the case of a noblewoman who murdered three husbands by incorporating *belladonna* berries into their meals, gradually increasing the dose to avoid detection. The final victim received approximately 15 berries crushed and mixed with wine, succumbing after a day of what appeared to be madness followed by coma.

Digitalis (foxglove): This is one of the more visually striking members of the witches garden. Though less dramatically poisonous in appearance than some of its counterparts, *Digitalis* contains cardiac glycosides whose therapeutic window is remarkably narrow. The medical use of *Digitalis* was formally introduced to mainstream medicine by William Withering in 1785, though folk herbalists had employed it for centuries prior. Used primarily for 'dropsy' (oedema resulting from congestive heart failure), foxglove tea was prepared using a single dried leaf (approximately 0.1–0.2 grams) steeped in hot water, administered once daily for no more than a week. The Welsh Physicians of Myddfai, whose medical texts date to the

13th century, described foxglove preparations for the treatment of headaches and to 'strengthen the heart rhythm'. Their dosage was remarkably precise — no more than half a fresh leaf (approximately 0.3 grams) infused in wine, taken in three divided doses over 24 hours. In Celtic tradition, foxglove was associated with the fae realm, its name in Welsh, Maneg Ellyllon, translates to Good People or Fairy Glove. There are several protective spells incorporating foxglove, particularly those intended to shield children from being replaced by changelings. A common practice involved placing a single foxglove flower above the cradle, never allowing the child to touch or consume any part of the plant.

The 16th-century grimoire *Le Dragon Rouge* includes foxglove in a complex ritual for divinatory purposes, wherein the practitioner would wear a garland of the flowers whilst seeking visions. The text specifically warns that no part of the plant should touch bare skin, suggesting an awareness of its toxic properties even when used externally.

In Cornish folklore, foxglove was believed to amplify any spell cast during the full moon, particularly those related to matters of the heart — both romantic concerns and physical ailments of the cardiac system. The narrow therapeutic window of *Digitalis* makes it particularly dangerous, with the consumption of 2–3 grams of dried leaf material being enough to induce fatal cardiac arrhythmia. Death comes through disruption of the heart's electrical conduction system, often manifesting as a paradoxical slowing of the pulse followed by deadly acceleration and fibrillation.

Hemlock *(Conium maculatum):* Bearing delicate white umbels reminiscent of Queen Anne's Lace, hemlock's appearance belies its deadly nature. The plant contains coniine and other piperidine alkaloids that produce progressive paralysis whilst leaving the mind chillingly intact. Despite its extreme toxicity, hemlock found limited medical application as an antispasmodic and analgesic.

The Greek physician Dioscorides described the use of hemlock compresses (using approximately five grams of leaf material boiled briefly in water, then cooled) for the treatment of painful joints and inflammation. The preparation was never applied to broken skin.

Medieval Arabic medical texts document the use of highly diluted hemlock preparations (typically 0.05 grams of leaf extract in 30 millilitres of oil) for the treatment of neuralgic conditions and as a sedative for those suffering from mania.

Administration was strictly external, applied as a liniment to the temples and spine. Hemlock's association with boundaries, particularly the threshold between life and death, made it significant in necromantic practices. There are traditions from Eastern Europe wherein practitioners would place a small bundle of Hemlock leaves (never more than 3–4 leaves) beneath their pillow to facilitate communication with the deceased through dreams.

The plant features prominently in Greek magical tradition, where it was sacred to Hekate. The *Papyri Graecae Magicae* includes a ritual for divination requiring the burning of Hemlock stems (approximately one gram) as an offering to chthonic deities. Participants would carefully avoid inhaling the smoke, demonstrating awareness of the plant's toxicity even when not ingested directly.

Hemlock poisoning progresses with horrifying clarity for its victims. Ingestion of 6–8 grams of leaf material can prove fatal, with death resulting from respiratory paralysis whilst consciousness remains intact until the final moments. The paralysis ascends from the extremities toward the chest, eventually halting the diaphragm's movement. Socrates' death, as recorded by Plato, provides the most famous account of hemlock poisoning.

The executioner prepared a solution of approximately 70–100 grams of crushed hemlock seeds in wine, far more than necessary to ensure death.

Modern toxicologists estimate that the actual lethal dose would have been closer to 10 grams of seed material.

Datura Stramonium (thornapple): With its trumpet-shaped white flowers and spiny seed pods, *Datura* presents a striking appearance matched by its profound pharmacological effects. Containing scopolamine, hyoscyamine, and atropine, *Datura* induces potent hallucinations alongside dangerous physical symptoms. Traditional applications of *Datura* focused primarily on respiratory conditions. Nicholas Culpeper documented the practice of smoking *Datura* leaves (approximately 0.2 grams) mixed with tobacco for the treatment of asthma. The anticholinergic properties would indeed relax bronchial passages, though the practice carried significant risks.

In Ayurvedic tradition, which influenced certain European practices through trading routes, *Datura* seeds were incorporated into analgesic preparations for severe pain. The dosage was minuscule, no more than two to three seeds (approximately 0.05 grams) macerated in oil and applied externally to affected areas.

Perhaps no plant features more prominently in accounts of shamanic practice across cultures than *Datura*. Its use in European witchcraft for divinatory purposes and astral projection. A typical ritual might involve the consumption of a single seed (approximately 0.02 grams) or the application of a *Datura*-infused ointment to the temples. The *Book of Oberon,* a 16th-century grimoire, contains a formula for scrying requiring the burning of *Datura* flowers (approximately 0.5 grams) as an incense during ritual work. Practitioners were cautioned to work only in well-ventilated spaces and to avoid direct inhalation of the smoke.

In southern European tradition, *Datura* was associated with prophetic dreams when a single flower was placed near (never under) the pillow. The scent alone was believed sufficient to induce visionary states, though modern understanding suggests that this would be unlikely without actual consumption or absorption of the plant's constituents. *Datura's* toxicity is considerable. Consumption of 15–25 seeds (approximately 0.3–0.5 grams) could prove fatal, particularly in children or the elderly. Death results from hyperthermia, cardiac arrhythmia and respiratory depression often occur after a period of violent hallucinations.

The 17th-century *Compendium Maleficarum, which was a witch hunters manual,* records several cases of apparent *Datura* poisoning, including an account from Milan wherein a family of five died after consuming bread contaminated with *Datura* seeds. Autopsy findings described extreme dilation of the pupils, dryness of the mouth, and evidence of self-inflicted injuries sustained during hallucinatory episodes.

The key to working with Hekate is liminality: my moon gardens provide the space for ritual, contemplation, and learning. They also provide me with ingredients for potions and magical work while connecting my practice to the ancient traditions of botanical magic. Through understanding plant properties and energies, I can augment spells and rituals with botanicals that complement their intended purposes.

My work within the gardens reflects how modern practitioners can honour ancient traditions while adapting them to contemporary life. The spaces connect me directly to both earth-based practices and honouring my ancestors. This forms the foundation of magical work, showing how the power to heal or harm truly lies at our fingertips in the soil we tend.

Please don't try any experimental dosing of dark botanicals, these explanations are only intended for information purposes, and I really don't want to get arrested for assisting in mysterious murders...

THE RITES OF HEKATE

Do you ever wonder what the difference is between a rite and a ritual?

I often hear them used interchangeably.

To clarify, a rite is an established and well-structured ceremonial act. Rituals are the actions that are performed in a rite with a symbolic meaning. Most of what I am talking of in this chapter are rites, but within them there are several rituals, such as offering food and libations, chanting and moving and the lighting of candles or torches.

Today you can find many suggested rites relating to Hekate, they come in very different forms. In this chapter I am sharing some of the rites that I know and practice. Clearly, I am not providing 'recipes'. I have not included all of my own practice, but enough for people to adapt and adopt rites and rituals for themselves.

Much of my own work is based on research from older texts such as the Greek Magical Papyri, and there are many people that have done excellent research just in case your ancient Greek, or Coptic is not that hot. I suggest if you are serious, then you need to undertake your own research and find your own path. One question you might begin with is: where should rites take place?

A clue to this lies in history. As we know, by the 5th century BCE, Hekate had become firmly associated with crossroads, particularly the triodoi three-way crossroads, where her Hekataia were regularly placed. By our house is our own intersection of three roads. The triple crossroads is particularly powerful in magical practice; its relevance and uses maybe ancient but still survive today. Although I have to compete with my neighbour's shrine to the Madonna, it's one of the places where I undertake some of my rites.

Before taking a dive into rites, it's worth just thinking about your purpose and practice. By this, I am referring to the magickal practices of invocation and evocation, which represent two fundamentally different approaches to working with spiritual entities, energies and powers. The two words are often used interchangeably in casual conversation. However, they entail distinct methods and purposes that any serious practitioner ought to understand. These distinctions have deep roots in Western esoteric traditions, so if you want to learn more, which I strongly recommend, you could look at some of the following: The Golden Dawn system, as documented in Israel Regardie's *The*

Golden Dawn (1937–1940), clearly differentiates between invocation and evocation in its ritual structures, with specific protocols for each practice. Aleister Crowley explores these concepts extensively in *Magick in Theory and Practice*, describing invocation as 'the bringing in or identification with a certain deity or spiritual essence' while evocation involves 'the summoning of a being...into visible appearance'. John Dee and Edward Kelley's Enochian system, as recorded in Dee's journals from the 16th century, provides some of the most detailed historical accounts of ceremonial evocation practices in Western occultism. Traditional British cunning folk, as documented in Owen Davies' *Popular Magic* (2003), often practised forms of evocation when working with spirits, keeping clear boundaries between practitioner and entity. In contemporary practice, Emma Restall Orr's *Druidry* (2007) offers valuable perspectives on invocation as a sacred invitation within modern pagan traditions, emphasising relationship rather than hierarchy.

In this distinction, the word 'invocation' comes from the Latin 'invocare', meaning 'to call within'. This refers to the act of calling a spiritual force, deity, or energy into oneself. When invoking, the practitioner becomes a vessel, or channel, for the invoked entity or power.

The essence of the invoked force temporarily merges with the practitioner's consciousness and body. Crucially, invocation is better understood as an invitation rather than a demand. As Dion Fortune notes in her work *The Mystical Qabalah,* invocation involves 'the drawing down of force or consciousness from a higher plane' through reverent appeal and receptivity. She identifies three forms of connection.

The first, Reverent Appeal, is addressing higher powers or entities with respect and reverence, recognizing their authority and importance. This involves not just making demands but expressing humility and sincerity in your request. Receptivity is the importance of being open and receptive to the influence of the higher plane. This means cultivating a state of inner stillness and a willingness to allow the force or consciousness to flow into you. It's not about forcing the process, but about creating the conditions for it to happen. Drawing Down refers to the process of actively seeking and attracting a higher power or consciousness into one's own being. This can be through ritual, meditation or simply through cultivating the right inner attitude.

The practitioner creates a sacred space where the divine may choose to manifest, rather than attempting to compel its presence.

This approach of respectful invitation acknowledges the agency and dignity of the spiritual forces with which we work. During a successful invocation, you might experience altered states of consciousness, or a sense of expanded awareness. Sometimes, I have witnessed personality shifts reflecting attributes of the invoked force. There is also the potential for enhanced abilities associated with the invoked entity, and if successful, this can lead to profound insights or divine inspiration. An example of invocation could be when a priestess might invoke the goddess Cerridwen, to access her wisdom and powers of transformation during a ritual. The priestess temporarily embodies aspects of the goddess, speaking with her voice and channelling her energy. This communion allows the priestess to gain a deeper understanding and manifest the goddess's qualities in her workings.

Evocation, on the other hand, is from Latin 'evocare', meaning 'to call forth'. It involves summoning an entity or energy to appear externally, separate from the practitioner. The evoked force manifests outside the magician's body, often within a predetermined space such as a magick circle or triangle. An evocation maintains clear separation between the self and the evoked force. It is based on making a direct command rather than invitation. It is therefore possible to observe and interact with the entity as distinct from oneself and is often used to employ protective measures. The 1st century CE Roman poet Lucan, in his epic *Pharsalia*, describes how necromancers would call upon Hekate to allow communication with these spirits. Despite their fearsome reputation, the spirits of Hekate's Horde also play a critical role in evocation.

The PGM contain several spells that seek to harness these entities as supernatural assistants. For example, the first two spells in the PGM I detail a ritual to gain a 'spirit assistant' (paredros). Another practice is where a practitioner would approach a crossroads at night, make specific offerings, and attempt to capture one of these spirits to perform magical tasks.

Before trying out a ritual, it is always necessary to consider protection. In our own home, I have witnessed Nat be attacked by a daemonic type of entity that left him with a burn and scar on his arm. Protection comes in several forms. There is protection of yourself from conscious or unconscious attack, both physical and mental. There is also the need to create your ritual space so you both invite energies or spirits in, but also give them the opportunity to leave, rather than leaving something hanging around, which can get you into all kinds of trouble.

If you are relatively new to this kind of work, you also need to be able to recognise the trickster element; just because you think you have evoked Hekate, it does not mean it is her you are actually communing with. In terms of my own protection practice, Jason Miller's book, *Protection and Reversal Magic,* is invaluable, and a good starting point for thinking about how to create protection over your spaces and for yourself. The other go-to book is Caitlin Mathews' *The Psychic Protection Handbook*, again very practical and common sense. Both authors, although taking very different approaches, start with the same premise that a positive, strong and healthy mind helps a lot when you are doing this sort of work. So, begin with exercises where you practice positive affirmations, self-talk and develop your sense of self-worth. It sounds easy, but is not. This requires regular reflection and challenging old and outdated views that you have of yourself or that others impose upon you. It is only once you have worked on a strong sense of self, have created a positive and protected space and your own methods of opening and closing your space, that I believe you will be ready to start with rituals. Some of the rituals I show here have evolved significantly over time. Hekate's worship transformed from temple to primarily household practices to increasingly sophisticated magical operations.

This evolution corresponded with Hekate's changing role in the Greek pantheon, from a household goddess of boundaries to a powerful mistress of magic with underworld associations.

Hekate's rituals have incorporated elements of diverse magical systems while maintaining their fundamental Greek structures. The continued archaeological discovery of curse tablets and protective amulets invoking Hekate demonstrates the practical application of these rituals across the Mediterranean world. Contemporary practitioners working within these historical frameworks understand that these rituals represented aspects of ancient Greek sacred and magical worldviews rather than isolated practices. They formed part of a cosmological system in which maintaining good relationships with divine forces was essential for both individual and community wellbeing. The rituals in the PGM served various magical functions. Firstly, there are divinatory rituals, such as the dream oracle in (PGM VII.222–249), which sought prophetic dreams. Very common are curse tablets and binding spells, like those in PGM IV.2441–2621, which is a spell of attraction. Finally, the creation and use of protective spells, described in PGM LXX.4–25, were designed to ward off punishment and evil influences from the underworld.

In terms of my own practices, I adapt to modern life and my own values and beliefs. For example, one particularly complex ritual found in PGM IV instructs the practitioner to create a special ink for writing magical formulae by combining myrtle, wormwood, styrax, and black Nubian dirt with the 'blood of a goat that has been quartered whilst facing the sunrise'. This substance was then used to inscribe clay tablets with invocations.

There are also many rituals that required the sacrifice of a black dog or the head of a black dog. Personally, I am never going to do that, but there are also examples of black dogs being moulded from wax and left at crossroads. It's perfectly acceptable to adapt rituals (for the dog's sake let alone your own). For me, the ritual must require the effort and respect required to affect change. I don't believe the 'blowing candles and making a wish' as a serious or effective form of magickal practice, but nor am I interested in sacrificing other animals or people.

The Magical Efficacy of Voces Magicae
The voces magicae ('magical voices' or 'words of power') found within ancient magical texts like the Greek Magical Papyri, represent far more than mere historical curiosities. They are potent magical technologies with profound implications for contemporary practice.

The consensus regarding these voces magicae suggests that they were deliberately constructed to resist conventional translation, and they are often combined elements from multiple languages (Egyptian, Greek, Hebrew). There are three broadly different schools of thought about how to employ the voces magicae.

The first contends that that precise vocalisation was is essential in certain traditions. In fact, many magical papyri include specific pronunciation guides. This might suggest that the sound rather than the semantic meaning of these formulae was considered most important. This perspective views magical language as operating through sound vibrations that interact with the cosmos in specific ways, rather than through symbolic meaning. This phonological perspective asserts the sounds themselves were thought to be potent, not the meaning of the words. Supporting this argument is the prevalence of palindromes and vowel sequences in magical texts as evidence that the sonic qualities of these utterances were paramount. From this perspective, the voces magicae function as direct vibrational keys to specific spiritual frequencies. When you intone sequences like MASKELLI MASKELLŌ PHNOUKENTABAŌ (from PGM IV 3172-3208) you're not simply reciting nonsensical syllables but engaging with sound patterns that ancient practitioners discovered could alter consciousness and facilitate direct communion with divine powers. These formulations operate beyond the limitations of ordinary language, as they bypass the rational mind and logical frameworks that can inhibit magical workings. Contrary to this view is the idea that magical language operates primarily through its performative qualities rather than its phonetic ones. From this perspective, the issue is not whether magical spells are meaningless but whether their efficacy depends upon deep and subtle understanding of the meaning.

From this perspective, the power of magical language derives from its ritual context and performative intention rather than precise pronunciation. Supporting this view, and from the analysis of Christian magical texts, is the argument that the unintelligible nature of magical words may be part of their function. This signals the extraordinary nature of the communication taking place. This would suggest that the alien quality of magical language is itself significant, serving to mark a departure from ordinary discourse. The debate becomes more complex when considering traditions where magical words were understood to derive from ancient or divine languages. In some rituals, practitioners said their words derived from the language of the gods or other primordial tongues.

In such cases, attempts at correct pronunciation might be seen as efforts to approximate divine speech patterns. Archaeological evidence complicates matters further; analysis of lead tablets and papyri shows magical inscriptions with spelling variations within the same formula, suggesting either that exact orthography and by extension, pronunciation, was not crucial, or that magical practitioners had different understandings of a correct form. Their power lies in their resistance to intellectual analysis, creating a bridge between human consciousness and divine presence through sound rather than meaning.

Some contemporary ceremonial magicians place great emphasis on precise pronunciation. Israel Regardie, in his influential works on ceremonial magic, insisted that the vibration of God-names and words of power required specific techniques for maximum effect.

The Greek Magical Papyri often include detailed phonetic instructions, although it's not always clear what sound a baboon or a shepherd makes. Medieval grimoires sometimes seem more concerned with the visual representation of magical words than with their vocalisation. This suggests that the importance of pronunciation may vary, depending on the specific magical system in question.

From a practical standpoint, voces magicae certainly create profound alterations in your neurological state during ritual. The repetition of unfamiliar sound patterns disrupts ordinary patterns of thought, facilitating the shift from mundane to magical consciousness. This neurological disruption is precisely what enables the deep trance states necessary for advanced magical work. When you learn to intone these formulations, particularly with the rhythmic patterns and tonal qualities suggested in sources like the PGM, you are temporarily 'rewiring' your consciousness to become receptive to dimensions of reality typically filtered out by ordinary perception.

These are not formulations to be approached casually. The voces magicae represent concentrated magical technologies developed and refined over centuries of practice. When properly employed, they can dramatically accelerate your magical development and deepen your connection to Hekate, but they demand preparation, respect, and proper ritual context to function as intended.

For me, probably the most powerful ritual we have undertaken was a fire ritual. I don't want to go into too many details, but we had experienced a particularly nasty attack, which had taken many forms. It's important to make this distinction, as when undertaking rituals that are either asking for protection or Karma acceleration from an unjustified attack, it's necessary to reflect on your own contributions and check that justice does not need to be metered out to you too. In this particular instance it really was an attack based on greed and envy. We undertook a ritual to petition for both protection and justice.

The ritual took place in the moon garden and after we had completed it, Nat took some photographs of the remaining fire. We were both surprised to see the results. The photograph has not been doctored or 'enhanced' in any way. No chemicals were used to change the colour or nature of the fire. What we saw in the photograph shown here, was what was present during the ritual.

Paracelsus (1493–1541), in his work *Liber de Nymphis, Sylphis, Pygmaeis et Salamandris et de caeteris spiritibus* (A Book on Nymphs, Sylphs, Pygmies, and Salamanders, and on the Other Spirits, c. 1530), described salamanders as beings composed entirely of the element of fire, dwelling within flames and volcanic regions.

Unlike the classical notion of salamanders as merely fire-resistant creatures, Paracelsus conceived of them as actual inhabitants of the fire element, parallel to how nymphs inhabited water, sylphs the air, and gnomes the earth. He argued that each element possessed its own form of life, and salamanders represented the highest and most volatile of these elemental beings due to fire's transformative nature. Paracelsus believed salamanders were generally invisible to ordinary human perception but could occasionally manifest during magical operations. Salamanders served as intermediaries between the spiritual and material realms, embodying the purifying and transformative properties of fire itself.

Needless to say, the ritual was powerful, the results were what we desired, and the photograph is the surviving evidence of the power of rituals when well prepared and undertaken.

The 'When and Where' of Rituals
There are often specific instructions regarding the lunar timing of rituals dedicated to Hekate. For example, the Deipnon is carried out on the night of the dark moon, during the hour after twilight.

Along with the appropriate timing, there are often detailed instructions for where rituals ought to be performed. The crossroads is a most obvious one, but there are others too.

Some involve creating a sacred space, which might be a triangle, or an altar-type space. In my practices these often involve the burial of magical items or the recitation of invocations to Hekate. There is a crossroads ritual based on taking a triangular shard from a place where three roads meet, and to then write with myrrh ink the names of Hekate. Go to a crossroad at the first hour after sunset. Place the shard upon the ground. Make an offering of wild thyme. There are also often specific instructions about using herbs in conjunction with lunar phases such as: 'Gather the sacred herbs as the moon wanes, speak her names thrice, and place them at the three-way crossroads. Return at dawn.'

The Deipnon
Probably the most well-know of all Hekate's rituals is the Deipnon, or Hekate's Supper. As the ritual marking the end of the lunar month, it functions as both a sacred observance and a practical means of household purification. The Deipnon would offer protection for a household between one lunar cycle and the next. Households performed this ritual primarily to appease Hekate and the restless dead, known as Hekate's Hordes, who wander with her. By leaving food at crossroads, practitioners create a buffer zone of protection, distracting potentially harmful spirits from entering their homes.

The offerings were meant to satisfy both Hekate and her ghostly retinue, preventing them from bringing misfortune to the household. The specific foods offered (garlic, eggs, fish, bread) held symbolic importance. Garlic is widely considered to have protective qualities, and eggs represent potential and transition, appropriate for the liminal time between lunar months. The entirety of the ritual, from the thorough house cleaning to the careful placement of offerings, creates a complete system of protection and purification.

The ritual is traditionally performed during the dark moon. I use this ritual to venerate Hekate and give thanks to the positive and nurturing things in my life, but also to reflect on how I am in the world and consider what I need to put right, which is the atonement aspect of the ritual.

This ritual is a good place to start if you are contemplating journeying with Hekate. The following is my adaptation but based on serious research and reflection. I am vegan, so I don't leave any animal derived products, and being conscious of the environment I don't leave anything that I think will cause damage. I also hate aluminium or plastic tea light holders, which today seem to be scattered across many sacred sites.

Step-by-step Deipnon Ritual

Purpose: Protection, veneration and atonement (as a part of personal growth)

When: This ritual is undertaken during the dark moon phase each lunar month. It is done in first hour after dusk. I aim to do it every month although it's not always possible.

1 Clean and purify your home, or something, even if small, thoroughly before the dark moon.

2 Prepare a simple meal including traditional foods such as eggs, garlic, leeks, fish, bread and cakes. At twilight, when you have prepared and opened the sacred space you are using, you can say something along the lines of this:

'At the dark of the moon, when shadows lengthen and the boundary between worlds may be traversed, I prepare this sacred offering for Hekate, Mistress of Crossroads, Guardian of Liminal Spaces. Hearken, Goddess of the Torches, Queen of the Night, Thou who walkest between the worlds, who hearest the whispers of spirits and the silent prayers of mortals. I come before thee with reverence, bearing the ancient offerings as our ancestors did in times long past.'

It doesn't have to be in Shakespearean English. Find whatever works authentically for you.

3 Expiation:
'Hekate, I atone for my wrongdoings in the last moon cycle, this includes...' Say out loud your wrongdoings. Be honest and use it as a moment for reflection and genuine atonement.

4 Make The Offering:
'This Deipnon, this supper, is thy sacred meal, prepared with intention and respect. We place before thee food and libations, both pure and purposeful. These are the traditional offerings that have called thee forth since the days of ancient Aegean nights.

Let the crossroads be thy altar, the moonless sky thy canopy. Accept these gifts as we remember thy power: thou who guides souls, illuminates darkness, and stands at the threshold of all transformations.'

My offerings do not include fish, eggs, meat or cheese, as I am vegan, but do include dandelions (both leaves and flowers), pomegranate seeds and pine nuts and bread or cakes, which I make myself. I also add a pinecone and a candle (never a tea light). I will often offer a drop of my blood as a part of the offering.

To do this I have a diabetic lancet, that I use to create one drop of blood and make sure it drops on the ground at the crossroads. You don't need more than one drop, to get a good drop of blood, make sure your hands are warm, shake them well to get good circulation and squeeze the top part of your finger before pricking it. If it's not forthcoming, wash your hands in hot water, shake them again and prick another finger. Giving your own life force is one of the most powerful actions you can undertake I don't support in anyway sacrificing others or other living creatures. It's not my way.

Place the food offering at a crossroads or at your property boundary. You can check online to find the exact hour of twilight and the transition from the dark moon to the new moon. Recite something like: 'Protect my household from malevolent spirits and accept this meal as token of respect.'

Close the ritual and avoid looking back after leaving the offering. Allow the offering to remain overnight.

As I said, we try and practice this ritual on every dark moon. On one occasion, Nat and I were undertaking the Deipnon ritual and just as we were closing our neighbour drove his motorbike into the middle of the crossroads, stopped his bike and said 'Ciao! What are you doing?' We laughed a lot, and I muttered 'Oh it's a Greek thing.' I suppose that's what happens at crossroads! So, yes, it's best to find a place that is quiet and secluded for this ritual, especially if you are intending to do it each lunar month and not be a further scandal to your neighbours.

Phosphoros Ritual (Light-Bearer Invocation)
The Phosphorous Ritual is probably a more modern construction. Whilst there are references to Hekate Phosphoros, there are no clear ancient references to this particular ritual (as far as I can tell).

Purpose: The Phosphoros ritual focuses on seeking Hekate's guidance and illumination. This ritual emphasises Hekate's celestial and illuminating aspects rather than her chthonic associations. The ritual is mainly used during periods requiring clarity, direction or during the initiation into certain mystery traditions.

I use this ritual when navigating difficult life transitions, and when I'm seeking clarity in confusing situations. I have also used this ritual when I begin new aspects of magical study or to enhance my psychic abilities and intuition.

When: The ritual's timing during the waxing or full moon phase aligned with Hekate's aspect as a bringer of increasing light and growing potential. The three candles represent Hekate's triple nature and her dominion over three realms. The walking pattern is three circumambulations, that establish a sacred space through which Hekate can manifest. This practice of creating sacred space through movement appears in many magical traditions, not only those related to Hekate but also in Dionysian and Eleusinian mystery rituals.

Step-by-step ritual:
1. Create an altar with three torches or candles arranged in a triangle (traditionally black, red, white).

2. Place symbols of Hekate's three realms: herbs (earth), incense (sky), and a bowl of water (sea).

3. Light torches or candles at sunset.

4. Walk three times deosil (clockwise) around the altar.

5. Meditate and ask for her guidance.

6. When finished close the circle, I tend to let the candles burn down.

Strophalos Ritual (Wheel of Hekate)
As previously discussed, the Strophalos is understood to be one of Hekate's most important magical tools, representing cosmic forces, cycles of time, and the power to transcend barriers between worlds. Although the origin of this ritual is unclear, it is understood to relate to the Chaldean Oracles and the PGM. Historical evidence suggests this ritual was primarily used by more advanced practitioners rather than in common household worship.

Unlike the communal or household nature of the Deipnon, the Strophalos ritual had more magical purposes in opening channels for divination, creating magical barriers against spiritual attack, facilitating soul journeys or underworld communications, and binding or releasing spells (depending on the direction of spinning). The spinning motion was thought to create a vortex of energy that could pierce the veil between worlds. This concept appears in multiple magical traditions around the Mediterranean basin, suggesting potential cross-cultural influences or shared magical technologies. The ritual's effectiveness depends on the practitioner's ability to achieve an altered state of consciousness while spinning the wheel.

Purpose: Theurgic practices, opening channels for divination, protection through creating barriers against magickal spiritual attack.

When: During liminal times (twilight, midnight) or during periods requiring protection or transition.

Step-by-step ritual:
1 To do this you need to create or obtain a Strophalos (Hekate's wheel symbol).

2 Anoint the wheel with protective herbs (traditionally mugwort, garlic, or lavender).

3 Hold the wheel at a crossroads or liminal space.

4 Turn the wheel deosil (clockwise) whilst chanting: 'Strophalos of Hekate, turn and bring her presence near. Guardian of the crossroads, triple-formed goddess appear.'

5 Meditate on the spinning motion, envisioning the boundaries between worlds blurring.

6 Place the wheel on your altar or carry it for continued protection.

Purification Rites

Purpose and significance: Purification rituals were fundamental to Greek sacred practice, but Hekate's specific purification had distinct characteristics focused on spiritual cleansing and the removal of miasma (ritual pollution or spiritual contamination).

These rituals were employed following: contact with death or corpses, after experiencing disturbing dreams or omens or misfortune and before undertaking other magical operations.

I regularly undertake a ritual bath before doing the Deipnon ritual. I add bundles of Hekate related herbs, (not the poisonous ones and to be honest, I don't add garlic! But I do add salt. The ritual bath represented both symbolic and practical cleansing. The specific herbs used had documented antimicrobial properties alongside their spiritual associations.

Apart from the ritual cleaning aspect there is also a symbolic submission, literally in submerging yourself whilst meditating. The complete immersion three times represents death and rebirth through water and is a common Mediterranean purification motif. The disposal of the bathwater at crossroads is particularly significant as it transferred the extracted negative energies to Hekate's domain, where she can transmute or disperse them.

When performed: As needed for purification, often at the dark moon

Step-by-step ritual:
1. Gather purifying herbs associated with Hekate (mugwort, garlic, lavender, dandelion).

2. Create a ritual bath with these herbs steeped in water.

3. Light three black candles around the bath.

4. Enter the water and immerse yourself completely three times.

5. While immersed, visualise negative energies being drawn out by Hekate.

6. Upon emerging, recite:

'Hekate Chthonian, Enodia, Trioditis, purify my body and spirit. As I pass through these waters, guide me through all crossroads.'

7. Allow yourself to air dry if possible.

8. Collect the bathwater and dispose of it at a crossroads after sunset.

This can be incorporated into your Deipnon ritual.

Kouria Hekates (Hekate's Provisions)
While the specific ritual designation of Kouria Hekates is not extensively documented in surviving classical sources, there is evidence that various provisioning rituals for Hekate existed alongside the better-known Deipnon. These practices appear to have varied significantly by region and time period, making it difficult to reconstruct a standardised version of this ritual from historical sources alone. While superficially similar to the Deipnon, this ritual serves a fundamentally different purpose. Traces of this ritual can be found in Hesiod's *Works and Days* and in Sophocles' fragment from *The Root-Cutters*.

Purpose and significance: Kouria Hekates established a reciprocal relationship seeking active guidance and divination. Seers and oracle priestesses often employed variations of this ritual before providing prophecies or conducting divination services for clients.

The creation of a hole in the earth established direct communication with the chthonic realm. The specific offerings chosen were believed to provide Hekate with the substances needed to manifest her oracular powers. Barley cakes provided sustenance, raw eggs represented potential and possibility, garlic offered protection and clarity, libations (honey, wine, and milk) are considered pleasing to underworld deities. This ritual is particularly employed by those seeking guidance at life crossroads or important decisions, for dreams or visions revealing hidden information, protection (particularly during dangerous journeys), assistance with legal matters or conflicts and help with fertility or childbirth issues. A period of silence following the invocation is crucial, as practitioners enter a receptive meditative state, often sensing Hekate's presence through sudden changes in temperature, unusual sounds or symbolic visions. These experiences would then be interpreted according to established divinatory frameworks.

When performed: During the waning moon, particularly when seeking guidance

Step-by-step ritual:
1. At a three-way crossroads, dig a small hole.

2 Place offerings of barley cakes, raw eggs, and garlic in the hole.

3. Pour a libation of honey, wine, or milk around the hole.

4. Light a black candle beside the offerings.

5. Recite the following invocation three times:

'Hekate Trioditis, guardian of the three ways, I offer these gifts in exchange for your guidance. Show me the path through darkness and illuminate my choices.'

6. Remain in silence for a period, meditating on your question or need.

7. Fill the hole after receiving guidance or at dawn.

In addition to ancient rites and rituals to venerate and celebrate Hekate, there are also modern-day practitioners such as Jason Miller, a contemporary occult author and practitioner, who has developed several protection rituals involving Hekate, based on his study of historical practices and his own magical system. If you don't already own a copy of his book, *Protection & Reversal Magick* , I would encourage you to buy a copy.

In addition, through her extensive writings and research, Sorita D'Este has significantly shaped modern understanding of Hekatean worship. Her book, *Hekate Liminal Rites* (co-authored with David Rankine), examines historical practices associated with the goddess, drawing from classical sources while making them accessible to contemporary practitioners.

D'Este's anthology *Hekate: Keys to The Crossroads* brought together diverse perspectives on the goddess from both scholarly and practitioner viewpoints, while her later work *Circle for Hekate* represents a comprehensive study of the goddess across historical periods. Cyndi Brannen is a contemporary witch, author and founder of The Keeping Her Keys mystery school and has developed numerous rituals involving Hekate with a particular focus on protection work. Her approach blends historical practices with modern witchcraft techniques, emphasising personal connection with Hekate through direct experience. One of Brannen's signature protection rituals involves creating a spiritual key of protection, drawing on Hekate's ancient association with keys as symbols of transition and access.

For me, part of developing a relationship with Hekate comes through both research and practice. I prefer older and verifiable sources but recognise that walking with your goddess does not mean you can only commune in ancient Greek standing atop a wind-swept mound with the remnants of a Greek temple casting a shadow, as lovely as that idea is. Modern practice is for modern practitioners dealing with modern issues.

AMONGST THE GRAVES AT NIGHT

'O triple-faced Hekate, virgin of the crossroads,
Light-bearer, heavenly one,
Mistress of the nether world, companion of the dark,
Night-wanderer, enemy of the light,
Friend and lover of solitude,
Rejoicing in the baying of hounds and in bloodshed,
Moving among the graves at night,
Thirsting for blood, bringing fear to mortals.

Porphyry (translated in Johnston Hekate Soteira p.140):

Hekate's association with necromancy is the essence of her connection to the chthonic realm. Necromancy, from the Greek terms 'nekros' (dead) and 'manteia' (divination), refers to the practice of communicating with the deceased to gain knowledge, particularly about the future. In the ancient world, this practice took several forms: consulting the spirits of the dead through ritual offerings, reanimating corpses to speak prophecies, descending to underworld locations to commune with spirits and summoning spirits to appear in dreams or vision.

Unlike modern horror-influenced conceptions, necromancy was, and still is, primarily concerned with acquiring hidden knowledge rather than raising armies of the dead (or at least I hope so). Hekate's association with necromancy developed gradually through several stages: In her earliest manifestations in Hesiod's *Theogony*, Hekate did not have any specific necromantic functions. Her necromantic aspects emerge more fully during the Classical and Hellenistic periods, as her chthonic associations deepened. By the 5th century BCE, Hekate became increasingly linked with crossroads, thresholds, and liminal spaces where she guides between worlds enabling both summoning and crossing over.

Necromancy was a method of communicating to gain knowledge, but there is also another method, which requires a journey to the underworld. This journey was called katabases. There are many famous examples of katabases in Greek mythology, for example Orpheus, who entered the underworld in order to bring Eurydice back to the world of the living, and Odysseus, who sought to consult with the prophet Tiresias.

Hekate was frequently in good company, of those who resided in the underworld but could also be called forth to the surface. Hekate has command of her own ghostly retinue known as the 'Horde of Hekate', also known as her 'train', 'retinue', or 'kōmos', and primarily consists of the restless dead and specifically, those souls unable to find peaceful rest due to untimely or violent deaths. Most of Hekate's Horde is made up of the spirits of girls and women who were judged to have died without honour. In heavily patriarchal societies this includes women and girls who died in childbirth, or as a result of sexual violence. It also includes prostitutes and women with 'loose morals', and of course, those practicing witchcraft. These women, and some men, were the murdered.

Also, amongst the retinue are the poor and those damned by society and who were denied proper burials. Reflecting this, there are four different categories within Hekates Hordes:

Those who died before their time (aōroi).
Those who died violently (biaiothanatoi).
The unmarried (agamoi).
Those who remained unburied (ataphoi).

These categories of the dead were considered particularly potent and dangerous because their life cycles had been interrupted prematurely. Hekate's hordes are often called upon in spells, even love spells to frighten the intended of the spell. Today we often think of Hekate's Hordes as something that is terrifying and remote but just think for a moment about the four categories.

Do you know someone who has passed on and falls into one of those categories — someone who died before their time or was unmarried, or who died violently? Do you imagine they could be a part of Hekate's Hordes?

One of the things that we know about Hekate's Hordes is that they often were the outcasts, maybe unloved and felt alone in their moment of death. What Hekate offered was to bring those into a group, to be a part of something and to feel unconditional love and protection.
Instead of seeing Hekate's Hordes as something terrifying and remote from us, maybe there is a moment to re-evaluate and even a realisation for me, that the lonely death of that woman from my regression, that opened this book, may have been welcomed into the Hordes, and finally belonged somewhere.

Among the few named entities associated with Hekate's spectral train, Mormo stands out as perhaps the most significant. Described as a frightening shapeshifter and female spirit, with horse-like features, she had been dead for a long period of time. Mormo was used to frighten children, who were told if they misbehaved, she would hide in their room and bite them. She appears in several ancient sources as a companion of Hekate.

Early references of Mormo include Xenophon's use of 'mormones' in his *Hellenica* (early 4th century BCE) to describe frightening masks, and a reference in Erinna's poem *The Distaff* (Ἠλακάτη) from around 350 BCE, mentioning 'Mormo with the swift feet'. One of the clearest references is in Theocritus' *Idylls* (15.40) from the 3rd century BCE.

Empusa is another named entity associated with Hekate's procession. Neither fully ghost nor demon but somewhere in between, the Empusa could supposedly shift between forms, often appearing as a beautiful woman before revealing a more monstrous aspect. Empusa has been used to refer to both a specific individual and a sub-group of daemons or demons. The 2nd century CE writer Philostratus, in his *Life of Apollonius of Tyana*, describes an encounter with an Empusa, noting that it 'belonged to the retinue of Hekate and was given to devouring bodies'. The figure's shapeshifting abilities made it particularly unsettling, embodying the liminal and transformative powers associated with Hekate herself.

The Lamiae, while not exclusively associated with Hekate, also appear in some accounts as part of her nocturnal retinue. These female entities were believed to seduce young men before consuming their flesh and blood.

The 3rd century CE philosopher Porphyry notes in his *Life of Plotinus* that certain types of spirits associated with Hekate 'whom others have called Lamiae and spectres of Hekate' could be summoned through particular rituals.

The horde manifested during the darkest hours of night, particularly at crossroads and liminal spaces. Their activity intensified during the dark of the moon and on specific nights sacred to Hekate. The spectral procession served multiple functions. Primarily, they acted as heralds of the goddess, announcing her divine presence. The 1st century CE Roman poet Lucan's epic *Pharsalia* contains a particularly vivid account of such manifestations during a necromantic ritual:

'The earth groaned as the Inachian goddess [Hekate] rose, followed by phantom forms. The barking of dogs told of her coming... ghostly shapes flitted about... and the boldest of magicians would have turned and fled had she not drawn her sword.'

Apart from her necromantic function, Hekate also had a role as a psychopomp, a divine guide of souls between the worlds of the living and the dead helping them navigate the complex and often dangerous journey to the afterlife. The term 'psychopomp' derives from the Greek ψυχοπομπός (psychopomps), combining ψυχή (psyche, 'soul') and πομπός (pompos, 'guide' or 'conductor'). Psychopomps possess certain characteristics that enable them to perform this crucial role, these include the ability to move freely between different realms, the mortal world, underworld and the celestial realm. They also require knowledge of the paths between worlds and can provide protection against the dangers of liminal spaces as well as retain authority that is recognised by both chthonic and celestial deities.

The earliest literary evidence for Hekate's role as a psychopomp comes from Hesiod's *Theogony* (circa 700 BCE), where she is described as having received honours and privileges from Zeus, including power over the earth, sea and sky. While this text doesn't explicitly mention her psychopomp function, it establishes her ability to move between realms which is clearly a crucial characteristic for a psychopomp. Also, Sophocles, in a fragment preserved by Plutarch, refers to Hekate as 'the one who holds the keys to the cosmos'. This epithet suggests her role in controlling passage between different realms, including the underworld.

The Homeric Hymn to Demeter (circa 7th–6th century BCE) provides more direct evidence of Hekate's role in guiding souls. In this text, she assists Demeter in searching for Persephone.

This text establishes her as a torchbearer, illuminating the way through darkness, a symbol that would become increasingly important in her psychopomp role. Hekate hears Persephone's cries when she is abducted by Hades and later serves as her companion and guide. This establishes Hekate's connection to both the underworld and the process of transition between realms. The *Chaldean Oracles* describe Hekate as a psychopomp, referring to her as the 'Soul-Mother' and 'Life-Generator' who guides souls during their descent into generation and their ascent after death. Although later than the classical Greek sources, these texts reflect earlier traditions and beliefs about Hekate's role.

Hekate's role as psychopomp is intimately connected to her association with crossroads, thresholds and liminal spaces. Ancient sources consistently place her at trivia (three-way crossroads), which were considered points of connection between the mortal world and the divine realms. Archaeological evidence, including numerous small shrines found at crossroads throughout the ancient Greek world, supports the literary sources' depiction of Hekate's connection to these liminal spaces. These shrines, known as Hekatea, often contained offerings and were particularly associated with nocturnal rites.

The specific aspects of Hekate's psychopomp function include guiding the recently deceased. Ancient funerary practices often involved invoking Hekate to guide the deceased's soul safely to the underworld. There are many examples of funerary inscriptions and the presence of triple-formed Hekate statues (Hekate trimorphos) in cemeteries and graves. As a protector against harmful spirits, Hekate not only guided souls but also protected the living from harmful spirits.

The PGM contains spells invoking Hekate for protection against restless souls and malevolent spirits. Hekate's role extended beyond simply guiding souls to the underworld. She also communicates between the living and the dead. There are several sources, including the PGM describe necromantic rituals involving Hekate. These practices often took place at crossroads or graves and involved invoking Hekate to facilitate communication with the dead.

As a psychopomp, Hekate was also associated with purification rituals, particularly those involving the cleansing of spaces or individuals affected by death. The *Chaldean Oracles* describe specific purification rites under Hekate's guidance.

Hekate's role as psychopomp is reflected in her tools and symbolic associations, perhaps the most important being the torch which represents Hekate's ability to illuminate the path between worlds. Ancient artwork consistently depicts her holding one or two torches, symbolising her guidance of souls through darkness. In addition to the torch, Hekate holds the keys to the cosmos, symbolising her ability to open passages between realms. Dogs are consistently associated with Hekate in ancient sources and have been described as her companions in guiding souls. Their ability to move between the wild and domestic spheres mirrors Hekate's own liminal nature. Vervain was specifically associated with Hekate's psychopomp role being used to open the gates between worlds. The method of preparation varied by region and specific use, but common practices included burning as fumigation, creating garlands, steeping in wine for libations, placing fresh vervain at crossroads and using in unguents for ritual participants.

Hekate's role as psychopomp influenced later religious and magical traditions. The medieval and Renaissance grimoire traditions often invoke her in this capacity, and her association with guiding souls has influenced modern interpretations of her worship.

The evolution of her psychopomp role can be traced through various historical periods. During the Classical period, Hekate's role as psychopomp was primarily focused on her function as a guide of souls and guardian of liminal spaces.

Archaeological evidence from this period includes the widespread presence of Hekate's shrines at crossroads throughout Greece. These Hekatea, as described by Aristophanes in his *Wasps* and *Lysistrata*, were sites of regular offerings and ritual activity The presence of dog bones and eggshells at these sites, as documented in archaeological reports, confirms the literary accounts of specific offerings associated with her worship. During this period, funeral practices regularly incorporated invocations to Hekate, as evidenced by funerary inscriptions found throughout Attica.

The Hellenistic period marked a significant evolution in Hekate's psychopomp role, characterised by increased syncretism and the development of more complex magical practices.

The Ptolemaic era saw her association with other underworld deities, particularly Isis in Egypt, as evidenced by the Greek Magical Papyri.

This period witnessed the development of more elaborate theological systems surrounding Hekate's role as psychopomp. *The Derveni Papyrus*, dating from this era, provides insights into how Greek mystical traditions interpreted her function in guiding souls. Her association with magic intensified, as demonstrated by the increasing number of spell tablets and curse tablets invoking her name in conjunction with underworld powers.

Archaeological records from this period shows an increase in the complexity of Hekate's iconography. Triple-formed statues became more common, and her attributes expanded to include keys, daggers and serpents, alongside the traditional torches. The Pergamon Altar's frieze, depicting Hekate in battle, demonstrates her elevated status in Hellenistic religious art. Theoretical works from this period, such as Apollonius Rhodius' *Argonautica*, present Hekate in an increasingly complex light, emphasising her role not just as a guide of souls but as a powerful mediator between worlds.

The development of mystery cults during this period also influenced her worship, with evidence suggesting initiation rites involving symbolic death and rebirth under her guidance.

The Roman period saw further evolution of Hekate's psychopomp role, characterised by synthesis with Roman deities and the development of more systematic magical practices. Hekate became increasingly associated with Trivia in Roman religion, while maintaining her Greek characteristics as a psychopomp.

The *Chaldean Oracles*, present perhaps the most developed theological system surrounding Hekate's psychopomp role. In these texts, she is portrayed as a cosmic soul-guide, responsible not only for guiding souls after death but also for their descent into material existence. Lucian's dialogues provide valuable insights into popular beliefs about Hekate's role during this period, particularly in his *Dialogues of the Dead*.

Archaeological evidence from Roman-era sites shows continued dedication of shrines at crossroads, though with increasing emphasis on her role in magical practices. The period saw the development of professional funeral guilds that incorporated Hekate's worship into their practices, as evidenced by inscriptions from Rome and other major cities. The PGM, though compiled during this period, preserves many earlier traditions while demonstrating how Hekate's role had evolved to include more complex magical operations.

The rites of Hekate provided structure for meaningful encounter with divine presence. It moves from the physical and foundational work of developing and tending the moon gardens to the more celestial connections. The exploration of necromancy does challenge contemporary discomfort with death whilst revealing it as one of Hekate's most profound gifts. In learning to commune respectfully with those who have crossed the threshold, we develop a more complete relationship with the cycles of existence. Death emerges not as ending but as transformation, with Hekate serving as guide through this space. This work teaches us that healing often requires facing what we fear most, and that wisdom often comes from sources beyond the living world.

FROM DIRT TO THE DIVINE

Today the understanding of Hekate continues to develop, with many different schools of thought writing, blogging or posting videos of how 'to do' Hekate.

The cloth of Hekate is woven by Classical scholars, historians, archaeologists, mythologists, pagans, Wiccans and many other magical practitioners, all offering their own version of Hekate. I have always rather liked John Dewey's example and description of a horse from different perspectives; a farmer, jockey, veterinarian and timid person will all perceive a horse in different ways and from different perspectives but still believe they are talking about the same conception. So, it is with Hekate; the classicist, Wiccan, archaeologist and modern magical practitioner each have their own view and understanding of Hekate and often have little interest in accommodating the 'truth' of others into their perspective. If you are open to the different perspectives and versions of the truth of Hekate, there is some important modern thinking that can be taken into consideration if you wish to further develop your own relationship with Hekate.

Sarah Iles Johnston's research of Hekate represents one of the most thorough modern analyses that has significantly influenced the understanding of Hekate in the last 30 years. Johnston portrays Hekate fundamentally as a liminal goddess. Her analysis reveals that Hekate's chthonic associations and connections to magic developed gradually rather than being intrinsic to her earliest manifestations. This perspective challenges the then prevalent view that Hekate was originally a chthonic deity. A significant contribution of Johnston's work is her examination of Hekate's evolution from ancient times through the Hellenistic era. She argues that Hekate's identity underwent substantial transformation, particularly during the classical period when she became increasingly associated with ghosts, necromancy and witchcraft.

In Hekate Soteira, Johnston focuses extensively on Hekate's representation in the *Chaldean Oracles*, highlighting her status in these later texts as a Cosmic World Soul. Johnston's analysis challenged many of the contemporary views of Hekate. In the late 20th century, many interpreted Hekate through the lens of her later magical associations, particularly as depicted in Neoplatonist and Roman literature and magical papyri. Johnston traces the development of Hekate's cult and worship over time, and in doing so, asserts that Hekate's identity remained fluid and adaptive, responding to broader cultural and religious shifts in the ancient Mediterranean world.

Johnston also reflected on Hekate's relationship to other deities. While earlier writers often presented Hekate as a marginal figure in the Greek pantheon, Johnston emphasises her important connections to Artemis, Persephone, and Demeter. Her analysis of the *Homeric Hymn to Demeter* identifies Hekate's role as a mediator between realms, which predated her later cosmic function in the *Chaldean Oracles*. Johnston's work also challenges a common assumption that Hekate was primarily a foreign import into Greek rituals and practices. While acknowledging possible Carian influences on her cult, Johnston presents Hekate as an integrated figure in Greek religious thought, whose evolution reflected internal developments within Greek religion rather than foreign inroads.

Johnston approaches Hekate as a goddess whose identity is continuously negotiated and renegotiated through ritual practice, literary representation and theological speculation. This perspective is in contrast to other interpretations prevalent in the 20th century, which often sought to identify an original or 'true' nature of the goddess.

In the decades preceding Sarah Iles Johnston's work, numerous scholars portrayed Hekate as a relatively marginal figure within the Greek pantheon, often subordinating her to other female deities or emphasising her foreign origins at the expense of her integration into Greek religious practice.

Lewis Richard Farnell set an early precedent for this viewpoint, describing Hekate as 'an alien goddess' whose worship represented 'a stream of religious influence flowing from Asia Minor'. This characterisation established a framework that many later 20th century scholars would adopt, positioning Hekate as peripheral to what they considered authentic Greek religious and magical practices.

Martin P. Nilsson, one of the most influential scholars of Greek religion in the mid-20th century, continued this trend in his *Geschichte der griechischen Religion*, where he acknowledged Hekate's presence in Greek religious practice but generally relegated her to a secondary status, particularly in his discussions of her relationships with Artemis and Persephone. He emphasised her chthonic nature and connections to magic while giving less attention to her other aspects, thereby reinforcing the image of Hekate as a somewhat peripheral deity concerned primarily with nocturnal and potentially dangerous domains.

Arthur Darby Nock typically centred his analysis on deities like Demeter, Artemis and Persephone, with Hekate appearing primarily in relation to these more prominent goddesses rather than as a significant figure in her own right. Jane Ellen Harrison, whose work on Greek religion often highlighted female deities and chthonic elements, tended to discuss Hekate primarily as an aspect or manifestation of the 'Great Goddess' rather than as a distinct deity with her own complex development and functions. In *Prolegomena to the Study of Greek Religion*, Harrison linked Hekate to pre-Olympian religious strata but often subsumed her individuality within broader patterns of goddess worship.

H.J. Rose, in his *Handbook of Greek Mythology*, which saw multiple editions throughout the 20th century, devoted significantly less space to Hekate than to other goddesses. When discussing her, Rose emphasised her connections to witchcraft and the supernatural, further cementing her reputation as a somewhat sinister, peripheral deity.

Walter Burkert's *Greek Religion*, a seminal work that shaped a generation of classical scholars, continued this tradition of treating Hekate as somewhat peripheral. While acknowledging her ancient origins, Burkert characterised Hekate primarily through her associations with boundaries, the 'uncanny' and magical practices. He wrote that 'Hekate remains an uncanny goddess' and emphasised her connections to 'ghosts and black magic' more than her other functions.

Karl Kerényi, despite his generally sympathetic treatment of Greek deities in works such as *The Gods of the Greeks*, similarly positioned Hekate predominantly as an addition to more central goddesses. His discussion of Hekate occurs primarily in his analysis of the Eleusinian Mysteries, where he treats her mainly as a companion to Persephone rather than as a deity with her own distinct mythological and cultic importance. Marcel Detienne further reinforced Hekate's perceived marginality in *The Gardens of Adonis*; he mentions Hekate, but again, mainly in relation to other deities and magical practices.

This trend of marginalising Hekate in scholarly literature began to transform with studies like Theodor Kraus's *Hekate*, which offered a more comprehensive examination of her cult and iconography. However, it was not until Johnston's work in the 1990s that a more multidimensional picture of Hekate emerged in contemporary scholarship, one that acknowledged both her connections to other deities and her independent significance in Greek religious thought and practice.

By the 21st century a new understanding of Hekate emerged in the works of people like Jason Miller, Cyndi Brannen, Jack Grayle, Sorita D'Este and David Rankine, who continue to shape our understanding of, and relationship with Hekate. All these people have influenced my own practice, and here I will provide a small summary of their approach, in the hope that it will inspire you to find out more and determine your own path for walking with Hekate. Beginning with Jason Miller; I understand his approach to Hekate as pragmatic, positioning her as a deity accessible to contemporary practitioners rather than an abstract theological concept. In his courses and writings, particularly those associated with his Sorcery of Hekate training programme, Miller presents Hekate as a multifaceted deity whose historical development and syncretism reflect her adaptability and ongoing relevance. Unlike approaches that seek to reconstruct a pure or original form of Hekate worship, Miller embraces the goddess's historical evolution and syncretism as evidence of her enduring power and significance across cultural and temporal boundaries. Miller advocates for what might be termed a 'historically informed innovation', where he acknowledges the historical and archaeological record whilst recognising the necessity of adapting ancient practices to contemporary contexts.

This perspective shares methodological affinities with the scholarly work of Sarah Iles Johnston, though directed toward practical application rather than purely academic enquiry. Central to Miller's conceptualisation of Hekate is what he terms the 'Crossroads Model', which interprets Hekate's dominion over liminal spaces not merely as a physical attribute but as a metaphysical principle. For Miller, the crossroads represent the intersection of multiple realms of existence, from the mundane world to the underworld, and the celestial realm. This tripartite understanding of cosmic structure corresponds to his tripartite understanding of Hekate herself, which he articulates as Hekate Chthonia (underworld/earth), Hekate Enodia (crossroads/middle world), and Hekate Ourania (celestial/upper world). This framework, while drawing inspiration from historical precedent, represents Miller's synthesis rather than a direct replication of any single ancient conception. Miller's tripartite model does not represent historical cult practice but offers a way for understanding Hekate's diverse attributes and functions. The model provides practitioners with a comprehensive framework that accommodates both the chthonic and celestial aspects of Hekate attested in various historical sources, from the *Theogony* to the *Chaldean Oracles*.

Miller's practical work with Hekate emphasises direct engagement through ritual, contemplative practice and what he terms 'spirit communication'. His methodology incorporates elements from diverse magical traditions. In *Protection & Reversal Magick*, Miller presents Hekate as a powerful apotropaic deity whose protection can be invoked against hostile forces. This work emphasises Hekate's role as a guardian of boundaries and her ability to turn back harmful influences. His Sorcery of Hekate programme expands this practical focus, presenting techniques for working with Hekate in various capacities: as psychopomp, as mistress of witchcraft, as cosmic intermediary, and as guide to spiritual development. The programme is notable for its integration of contemplative practices alongside more overtly magical workings, reflecting Miller's view that effective engagement with Hekate requires both ritual action and internal transformation. Miller employs what he terms a 'spirit model' of magic that allows for multiple interpretations of divine beings. This model accommodates psychological, energetic, and fully external conceptions of deity without privileging any single interpretation as definitive.

Cyndi Brannen has emerged as one of the most prominent contemporary voices on Hekatean practice, particularly through her influential books *Keeping Her Keys: An Introduction to Hekate's Modern Witchcraft* (2019), *True Magic: Unleashing Your Inner Witch* (2020), and *Entering Hekate's Garden: The Magick, Medicine & Mystery of Plant Spirit Witchcraft* (2020). As the founder of The Keeping Her Keys mystical witchcraft tradition and through her extensive writing on Patheos and her own platforms, Brannen has developed a distinctive approach to Hekate which resonates strongly with me and that blends historical awareness with psychological understanding and contemporary spiritual practice. At the heart of Brannen's work is her conceptualisation of a 'Modern Priestess Path' that makes ancient goddess worship accessible and relevant to contemporary practitioners.

Unlike approaches that focus primarily on historical reconstruction, Brannen's methodology emphasises personal connection, psychological integration and practical application of Hekatean wisdom in everyday life. For Brannen, working with Hekate isn't simply about performing rituals or studying ancient texts, it's about embodying aspects of the goddess and integrating her transformative power into one's life journey. This perspective is deeply informed by Brannen's background in psychology and her own profound personal experiences with the goddess.

What distinguishes Brannen's approach is her emphasis on Hekate as an accessible spiritual force for personal empowerment rather than a distant deity requiring elaborate propitiations. She presents Hekate as a guide through life's transitions and challenges, particularly accessible to women seeking to reclaim their power and sovereignty in a patriarchal world.

Central to Brannen's teaching is the symbolism of Hekate's keys, which she develops into a comprehensive framework for spiritual development and magical practice. Drawing on Hekate's ancient associations with keys to various realms, Brannen expands this metaphor into a series of 'keys' representing different aspects of personal and spiritual development: The Bone Key represents ancestral connections and shadow work. The Moon Key governs intuition, emotions and psychic development. The Serpent Key addresses healing, transformation and kundalini energy. The World Key connects practitioners to natural forces and elements, and the Cosmic Key opens awareness to universal consciousness and spiritual dimensions. For practitioners working with this system, these keys provide both a conceptual framework and practical tools for approaching different aspects of magical work with Hekate's guidance.

Each key corresponds to specific exercises, rituals, and areas of personal development that build upon one another to create a coherent spiritual practice. Complementing the keys system, Brannen presents Hekate's Three-Fold Path as a model for spiritual development. The Path of Fire focuses on personal empowerment, will, and transformation, The Path of Water develops emotional intelligence, intuition and healing and The Path of the Starry Road addresses higher consciousness and spiritual evolution. This tripartite structure echoes traditional associations of Hekate with the crossroads but reframes them in terms of spiritual development rather than physical locations. For practitioners, this offers a way to work systematically with different aspects of Hekate's energy according to their current needs and stage of development.

Unlike some approaches that present spiritual development as purely linear, Brannen's model acknowledges that practitioners may need to move between these paths throughout their journey, returning to fundamental work when new challenges arise or circumstances change. Brannen's *Entering Hekate's Garden* explores one of her most distinctive contributions to contemporary Hekatean practice: a comprehensive system of working with plant spirits under Hekate's guidance.

Drawing on historical associations between Hekate and various plants while incorporating contemporary herbalism and animistic practices, this approach offers practitioners a way to develop relationships with the botanical world as part of their devotion to Hekate. For the practical witch, Brannen provides detailed information on traditional Hekatean plants such as aconite, garlic, lavender, and mugwort, discussing their historical associations, magical properties, and practical applications. She goes beyond simple formulaic correspondences to encourage developing personal relationships with plant spirits through meditation, dreams, and direct communion. This approach is particularly valuable for practitioners seeking to ground their spiritual work in the natural world. Brannen's emphasis on ethical harvesting, and respect for plant spirits aligns with contemporary concerns about sustainability and ecological awareness. Drawing on her background in psychology, Brannen presents Hekate as a guide through the depths of the unconscious and a facilitator of shadow work, which is the process of acknowledging and integrating disowned aspects of the self. Brannen's *Keeping Her Keys* includes extensive exercises for confronting personal shadows, healing past wounds, and reclaiming personal power. She frames Hekate's traditional associations with the underworld not simply as literal connections to death and spirits, but as symbolic of the descent into the psyche required for genuine transformation. A recurring theme in Brannen's work is the reclamation of maligned feminine archetypes, particularly through her concept of the Modern Medea. Drawing parallels between the ancient sorceress Medea and contemporary women reclaiming their power, Brannen reframes this controversial figure as a symbol of feminine sovereignty and magical potency. This perspective speaks particularly to women who have experienced disempowerment or who are working to break free from patriarchal conditioning. Brannen presents Hekate as a guide through this process of reclamation, offering both compassionate healing and fierce encouragement to stand in one's truth and power.

The Modern Medea archetype also addresses the fear of women's anger and power that persists in contemporary society, offering practitioners a framework for understanding and channelling these energies constructively rather than suppressing them. Brannen has developed several ritual cycles for working with Hekate throughout the year, most notably her Sacred Seven ritual series, which aligns with lunar cycles and seasonal transitions.

These structured approaches provide practitioners with a sustainable, ongoing framework for devotion rather than isolated workings. Her emphasis on consistent devotional practice, which includes simple daily acknowledgments alongside more elaborate ritual work, encourages practitioners to develop a relationship with Hekate that extends beyond crisis moments or specific magical needs. This relationship-centred approach reflects Brannen's understanding of deity work as a reciprocal exchange rather than a transactional interaction.

Jack Grayle's work represents a synthesis of ancient Mediterranean magical traditions with modern devotional practice centred on Hekate. His approach is fundamentally grounded in the magic of late antiquity and draws principally from the Greek Magical Papyri, classical literature and Mediterranean mythology to construct a coherent system of Hekatean practice. Grayle's foundational premise is based on his belief that 'the best-preserved magical tradition in the West is found in the Greek Magical Papyri (PGM)', This perspective positions his practice not as a reconstruction of ancient religion but rather as a continuation of the syncretic magical traditions from the Hellenistic and Roman periods. He presents Hekate through the triple aspect of Maiden-Serpent-Wolf, emphasising her liminal nature as one who 'embodies the very thresholds that stand between realms'. This conception aligns with her traditional roles as psychopomp, Chthonic deity, and guardian of crossroads, but also incorporates the more complex theological developments found in the magical papyri where she appears as a World Cosmic Soul principle governing transformation and passage between states of being.

Grayle describes *The Hekataeon* as a Hymnal to Hekate: 'an ecstatic work dedicated to the Maiden-Serpent-Wolf and manifested by her divine grace'. He presents his work as 'forged by the author's personal journey, as a grimoire that maps out a series of serpentine windings that lead the reader through a labyrinth of songs, spells, chants, and invocations'.

The structure is based on an initiatory progression, reflecting Grayle's conception of Hekatean practice as a transformative spiritual journey rather than merely a collection of magical techniques. The contents of *The Hekataeon* reflect this synthetic approach through what appears to be a comprehensive initiatory system.

The work presents rituals, rites, spells, songs, scripts and sorcerous workings to ally oneself with Hekate as well as working with Medea, Kirke and Pasiphae energies.

This expansion beyond Hekate reveals Grayle's understanding of these a broader current of chthonic magical practice rather than merely discrete entities. The practical orientation of Grayle's work is evident in his teaching activities, where he offers courses in PGM practice and Hekatean devotion.

Sorita d'Este has dedicated over two decades to researching, writing about, and working with Hekate. Her works include *Hekate Liminal Rites* (co-authored with David Rankine, 2009), *Bearing Torches: A Devotional Anthology for Hekate* (2010), *Circle for Hekate* (2017-2018), and *Hekate: Goddess of Witches* (2020). D'Este has shaped how contemporary practitioners approach Hekatean magic and devotion. As the founder of the Covenant of Hekate, an international community of devotees, her influence extends beyond her writings to the development of living traditions of practice. Her research draws on classical texts, archaeological findings, historical accounts, and anthropological studies, examining Hekate across different time periods and geographical locations. This allows practitioners to understand the historical development of Hekatean worship from its earliest examples through its evolution in Greek, Roman, and Byzantine contexts, and finally to modern interpretations.

Her books typically include both historical analysis and ritual techniques, prayers, and practices that contemporary devotees can incorporate into their work. This balanced approach allows practitioners to ground their practice in historical understanding while adapting traditions for modern contexts. Central to d'Este's conception of Hekate is her emphasis on liminality and the goddess's fundamental association with thresholds, boundaries, and in-between spaces.

In *Hekate Liminal Rites,* d'Este and Rankine examine how Hekate's dominion over crossroads symbolises her role as mediator between worlds and states of being. For magical practitioners, this perspective offers valuable insights into working with Hekate during times of transition or transformation. D'Este presents practical techniques for invoking Hekate at personal crossroads, career changes, relationship transitions, spiritual initiations as well as at temporal crossroads such as twilight, midnight, moon phases and seasonal shifts. This liminal framework also informs d'Este's approach to spirit work under Hekate's guidance. She offers methods for safely navigating the boundaries between the material world and spirit realms, drawing on historical practices while incorporating contemporary understanding of psychic protection and boundaries.

The metaphor of torch bearing, reflecting Hekate's traditional iconography with her twin torches, runs throughout d'Este's work and exemplifies her approach to spiritual tradition. She sees herself not as creating something entirely new, but as carrying forward the flame of ancient wisdom while illuminating new paths for contemporary practice.

My own system of working with Hekate is the path that spans from the darkest depths, reflecting Hekate's chthonic nature, to the highest celestial realms, reflecting her world soul aspects, taking us from our innermost psyche to the outer reaches of manifestation. This system organises the work along two axes: the vertical movement from earth to cosmos (from dirt to the divine), and the horizontal spectrum from internal to external workings. Through these intersecting dimensions, we create four quadrants of practice that together form a comprehensive approach to Hekatean magic. When we place these axes together, we reveal a map of spiritual development and magical practice that honours Hekate in Her complete sovereignty. As the goddess of crossroads, she presides over all intersections, including those between the mundane and divine, between our inner landscape and the outer world.

Each quadrant represents a distinct approach to working with Hekate's energies, yet all remain interconnected within Her web.

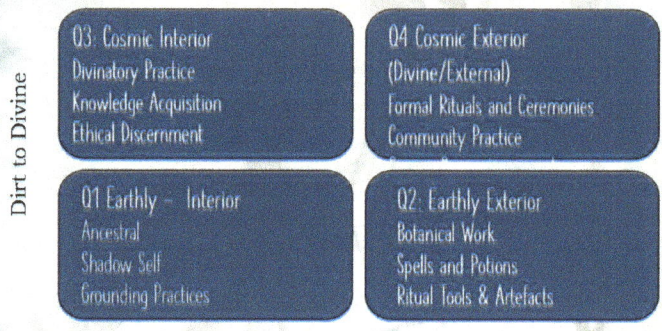

Internal to External

**The Quadrants of Hekatean Practice
Quadrant I:
Earthly Interior (Dirt/Internal)**
This quadrant concerns our relationship with our shadow aspects, ancestral connections, and personal psychological landscape. Here we address:

Psychological Shadow Work: Confronting and integrating our darker aspects under Hekate's guidance as She holds the torch that illuminates what lies beneath. This work involves journal practices, meditation with Her symbols (particularly the key and torch), and rituals of personal revelation.

Ancestral Connection: Establishing or strengthening bonds with those who came before us. Hekate as a Chthonic guide facilitates this communion through altar work, offerings and dream incubation techniques that open channels to ancestral wisdom. When I talk of ancestorial work, I am not just referring to our narrow bloodlines, but to a wider understanding of the different 'families' within which we grow. For example, when creating the moon garden, I purposely chose not to follow the definitions of each month's moon using an American or Native American system. It just does not resonate with me. Working with more European systems reflects my ancestry, where I have come from and what I understand. There are also groups that we elect into; be it a coven or a philosophical group that feels like 'home' and gives us a basis for our belief systems and understanding of our own sets of 'truths'.

Grounding Practices: Regular communion with the earth itself, barefoot walking, gardening as spiritual practice and meditation in natural settings to connect with Hekate's earthly aspect.

Quadrant II:
Earthly Exterior (Dirt/External)
This quadrant focuses on practical, manifest workings in the physical realm:

Botanical Workings: Cultivation of Hekate's sacred plants (yew, garlic, mugwort, etc.) and development of herbal preparations aligned with Her energies. This includes salves for protection, tinctures for dreamwork and botanical allies for crossroads magic.

Spells and Potions: Practical spell-craft addressing material concerns, protection of hearth and home, justice workings, and boundary establishment. All such workings incorporate elements of the chthonic realm (soil, roots, stones) with appropriate ethical foundations.

Ritual Tools and Artefacts: Creation and consecration of physical tools aligned with Hekate's earthly aspects — black-handled knives, keys forged at significant times, and vessels for offerings at physical crossroads.

Quadrant III:
Cosmic Interior (Divine/Internal)
This quadrant encompasses your relationship with Hekate's celestial and divine aspects as they manifest in your interior landscape:

Divinatory Practices: Development of intuitive abilities under Hekate's guidance, including scrying, dreamwork interpretation, and mediumship. These skills focus on receiving divine guidance for one's path.

Knowledge Acquisition: Dedicated study of Hekatean lore, historical practices and contemporary revelations. This includes academic study balanced with direct gnosis through meditation and contemplative practices.

Ethical Discernment: Development of a strong moral compass guided by Hekate's principles, particularly regarding the appropriate use of magical abilities for justice rather than revenge. This involves contemplative practices examining the difference between righteous action and egotistical reaction.

Quadrant IV:
Cosmic Exterior (Divine/External)
This quadrant addresses how Hekate's celestial aspects manifest through your external practice.

Formal Rituals and Ceremonies: Development of ceremonial workings that honour Hekate in Her celestial aspects, particularly at astronomically significant times. These might include full moon rites, devotions at Her traditional monthly festival (Deipnon) and seasonal observances.

Community Practice: Sharing Hekatean wisdom with others through teaching, ritual leadership, or community service projects that embody Her principles of guidance and protection at the crossroads of life.

Cosmic Connection Workings: Rituals that explicitly connect terrestrial practice with celestial energies, star magic, astrological timing of workings, and ceremonies that establish your role as intermediary between earthly and divine realms.

The Ladder System: Central to this approach is the concept of 'ladders' connecting the earthly to the divine. These ladders represent intentional pathways between quadrants, allowing for movement between different aspects of practice. Just as Hekate traverses all realms, so too may the practitioner move between different modalities of working with Hekate's energies.

The Ascending Ladder: Begin with grounding in earthly practice (Quadrants I and II) before ascending to cosmic workings (Quadrants III and IV). This ensures that divine connection remains rooted in practical reality.

The Integrating Ladder: Move deliberately between internal and external expressions (Quadrants I and III, or II and IV) to ensure that inner wisdom manifests in outer practice, and that external workings inform inner development.

The Crossroads Ladder: Periodically engage in practices that intentionally blend all four quadrants — these become your most powerful 'crossroads workings', where Hekate's fullest presence may be experienced.

Ritual Framework
Each significant working should acknowledge all four quadrants while emphasising the particular area of focus.

1 Begin with grounding and ancestral acknowledgment (Quadrant I).

2 Establish physical sacred space with appropriate tools and botanicals (Quadrant II).

3 Open to intuitive guidance and divine wisdom (Quadrant III).

4 Conduct the formal ceremonial aspects with cosmic awareness (Quadrant IV).

Personal Development Path
Your development as a Hekatean practitioner involves sequential proficiency of each quadrant while maintaining awareness of their interconnection.

1.Foundation Phase:
Emphasis on Quadrants I and II to establish strong earthly connection.

2. Expansion Phase:
Gradual incorporation of Quadrants III and IV while maintaining earthly practice.

3. Integration Phase:
Development of facility in moving between quadrants as needed.

4. Wisdom Phase:
Creation of unique workings that honour Hekate across all domains of practice.

Keeping the ego in check is a critical element of this system and involves constant vigilance regarding the role of ego in magical practice. Hekate guides us at the crossroads of motivation, helping us discern when we act from divine guidance versus personal desire. For each working, establish a 'three keys' assessment:

1. The Key of Necessity: Is this working truly necessary, or merely desired?

2. The Key of Consequence: Have all potential outcomes been thoroughly considered?

3. The Key of Authority: Does this working appropriately respect the autonomy of all involved?

Only when all three keys turn should the working proceed. This practice helps ensure that revenge never masquerades as justice, and that magical practice remains in service to higher principles rather than personal gain.

This system honours Hekate in Her complete sovereignty while providing a structured approach to developing a comprehensive magical practice. By recognising the importance of both earthly and divine aspects, both internal and external expressions, the practitioner creates a balanced relationship with this powerful goddess. The true magic lies not in any single quadrant, but in the practitioner's ability to move between them, ascending and descending the ladders that connect earth to cosmos, weaving together internal insight and external practice.
In this movement, we embody Hekate's essence as the goddess of transitions and crossroads, finding Her guidance in the spaces between.

This journey through the many faces of Hekate, from ancient goddess to contemporary guide, reveals her as a deity whose power lies not in remaining static but in her capacity for transformation. I have tried to share my personal experience along with some of the research I have undertaken about working with this goddess. In walking with Hekate through liminal spaces, I have found that the goddess of thresholds invites us to embrace transition as sacred, rather than something to be endured. Her presence transforms moments of uncertainty into opportunities for growth. For me, the creation of my moon gardens is an acknowledgement that I am constantly navigating thresholds: between sleeping and waking, between past and future, between who we have been and who we are becoming, and allows me to find the sacred in the ordinary transitions of daily life.

The moon gardens also reveal how spiritual practice can be grounded in the physical world through a conscious relationship with the botanicals that share Hekate's domain. The garden becomes a living shrine where the boundary between cultivation and devotion dissolves, reinforcing that spiritual practice need not be divorced from practical engagement with the natural world. Through plant partnerships, we learn that wisdom often emerges through patient tending rather than dramatic revelation.

What emerges from this exploration is the understanding that Hekate offers not answers but better questions. She teaches us to navigate uncertainty with courage, to find strength in vulnerability, to discover wisdom in darkness and to recognise the sacred potential inherent in every threshold we encounter.

Her gift lies not in removing the challenges of existence but in transforming our relationship to those challenges. In walking with Hekate, we learn to see crossroads everywhere: in career decision and relationship transitions, in moments of doubt and periods of growth, in the daily choices that shape character and the life-altering decisions that determine destiny. Under her guidance, every threshold becomes an opportunity for conscious choice, every limitation a boundary that might be transcended, every ending a potential beginning.

Hekate's blessing is not the promise of easy passage but the assurance that no threshold need be crossed alone. In her presence, every ending becomes a doorway, every question an invitation deeper into mystery, and every step forward an act of devotion to the sacred journey of becoming.

The work with Hekate never truly ends because transformation never ceases. As long as we face choices, encounter thresholds, and navigate the space between what is and what might be, her guidance remains relevant.

REFERENCES AND BIBLIOGRAPHY

Adams, P.M. (2017) The Game of Saturn: Decoding the Sola-Busca tarocchi. Bibliotheque Rouge
Albinus, L. (2000). *The House of Hades: Studies in Ancient Greek Eschatology.* Aarhus University Press.
Alvar, J. (2008). *Romanising Oriental Gods: Myth, Salvation and Ethics in the Cults of Cybele, Isis and Mithras* (R. Gordon, Trans.). Brill.
Antonangeli, R. (2024). Shelley's Prometheus Unbound and the Origins of Creation. In *Myths of Origins* (pp. 121-142). Brill.
Apuleius. (1989). *Metamorphoses* (J. A. Hanson, Trans.) Harvard University Press. (Original work published 2nd century CE)
Aristophanes. (2002). *Wasps. Lysistrata* (J. Henderson, Trans.). Loeb Classical Library.
Assagioli, R. (1965). *Psychosynthesis: A Manual of Principles and Techniques.* Hobbs, Dobson.
Athanassakis, A. N., & Wolkow, B. M. (2013). *The Orphic hymns: Translation, Introduction, and Notes.* Johns Hopkins University Press.
Barron, J. P. (1964). New Light on Old walls: The murals of the Theseion. *Journal of Hellenic Studies,* 84, 35-41.
Berg, W. (1974). Hecate: Greek or "Anatolian"? *Numen,* 21(2), 128-140.

Betegh, G. (2004). *The Derveni Papyrus: Cosmology, Theology and Interpretation.* Cambridge University Press.

Betz, H. D. (Ed.). (1996). *The Greek Magical Papyri in Translation, Including the Demotic Spells* (2nd ed.). University of Chicago Press.

Boegehold, A. L. (1999). *When a Gesture Was Expected: A Selection of Examples From Archaic and Classical Greek Literature.* Princeton University Press.

Bortolani, L. M. (2016). *Magical Hymns from Roman Egypt: A Study of Greek and Egyptian Traditions of Divinity.* Cambridge University Press.

Brannen, C. (2018). *Keeping her Keys: An Introduction to Hekate's Modern Witchcraft.* Moon Books.

Brannen, C. (2020). *Entering Hekate's Garden: The Magick, Medicine and Mystery of Plant Spirit Witchcraft.* Weiser Books.

Bremmer, J. N. (2014). *Initiation into the Mysteries of the Ancient World.* De Gruyter.

Burkert, W. (1985). *Greek Religion: Archaic and Classical* (J. Raffan, Trans.). Harvard University Press.

Burton, J. B. (1995). *Theocritus's Urban Mimes: Mobility, Gender, and Patronage.* University of California Press.

Butler, E. M. (1998). *The Fortunes of Faust.* Cambridge University Press.

Cancik, H., & Schneider, H. (Eds.). (2006). *Brill's New Pauly: Encyclopaedia of the Ancient World*. Brill.

Chrysostomou, P. (1998). *H Thessaliki Thea En(n)odia i Pheraia Thea* [The Thessalian Goddess En(n)odia or Pheraia Goddess]. Tameio Archaiologikōn Porōn kai Apallotriōseōn.

Churchill, C. (1994). *The Skriker*. Nick Hern Books.

Clay, J. S. (1984). The Hecate of the Theogony. *Greek, Roman, and Byzantine Studies*, 25(1), 27-38.

Clinton, K. (1974). *The Sacred Officials of the Eleusinian mysteries*. American Philosophical Society.

Clinton, K. (1992). *Myth and Cult: The Iconography of the Eleusinian Mysteries*. Svenska Institutet i Athen.

Cole, S. G. (1984). *Theoi Megaloi: The Cult of the Great Gods at Samothrace*. Brill.

Crowley, A. (1913). *The Rites of Eleusis*. The Equinox.

Crowley, A. (1929). *Magick in Theory and Practice*. Lecram Press.

Davies, O. (2003). *Popular Magic: Cunning-folk in English History*. Hambledon Continuum.

Dee, J. (1659). *A True & Faithful Relation of What Passed for Many Years Between Dr. John Dee and Some Spirits* (M. Casaubon, Ed.). T. Garthwait. (Original work 1582-1589) d'Este, S. (2017). *Circle for Hekate-Volume I, History & Mythology: Dedicated to the Light-Bearing Goddess of the Crossroads in All Her Many Faces, manifestations.* Avalonia.

d'Este, S., & Rankine, D. (2009). *Hekate Liminal Rites: A Study of the Rituals, Magic and Symbols of the Trch-Bearing Triple Goddess of the Crossroads.* Avalonia. [

Detienne, M. (1994). *The Gardens of Adonis: Spices in Greek Mythology* (J. Lloyd, Trans.). Princeton University Press. (Original work published 1972)

Dickie, M. W. (2003). *Magic and Magicians in the Greco-Roman world.* Routledge.

Dillon, M. (2002). *Girls and Women in Classical Greek Religion.* Routledge.

Duvick, B. (Trans.). (2007). *Proclus: On Plato's "Cratylus".* Bloomsbury.

Edmonds, R. G. (2019). *Drawing Down the Moon: Magic in the Ancient Greco-Roman World.* Princeton University Press.

Edwards, C. M. (1986). The Running Maiden from Eleusis and the Early Classical Image of Hekate. *American Journal of Archaeology*, 90(3), 307-318.

Euripides. (1963). *Medea* (R. Warner, Trans.). Penguin Classics. (Original work published ca. 431 BCE)

Euripides. (2002). *Helen, Phoenician Women, Orestes* (D. Kovacs, Ed. & Trans.). Harvard University Press.

Evelyn-White, H. G. (Trans.). (1914). *Hesiod, the Homeric Hymns, and Homerica.* Harvard University Press.

Faraone, C. A. (1991). Binding and Burying the Forces of Evil: The Defensive Use of "Voodoo Dolls" in Ancient Greece. *Classical Antiquity,* 10(2), 165-220.

Faraone, C. A. (2018). *The Transformation of Greek Amulets in Roman Imperial Times.* University of Pennsylvania Press.

Faraone, C. A., & Obbink, D. (Eds.). (1991). *Magika hiera: Ancient Greek Magic and Religion.* Oxford University Press.

Faraone, C. A., & Obbink, D. (Eds.). (2013). *The Getty Hexameters: Poetry, Magic, and Mystery in Ancient Selinous.* Oxford University Press.

Farnell, L. R. (1896). *The Cults of the Greek States* (Vol. 2). Clarendon Press.

Fauth, W. (1999). *Hekate Polymorphos: Wesensvarianten Einer Antiken Gottheit.* De Gruyter.

Foley, H. P. (1994). *The Homeric Hymn to Demeter: Translation, Commentary, and Interpretive Essays.* Princeton University Press.

Fortune, D. (1935). *The Mystical Qabalah.* Williams and Norgate.

Fraser, P. M., & Bean, G. E. (1954). *The Rhodian Peraea and Islands.* Oxford University Press.

Froud, B., & Windling, T. (1998). *Good Faeries/Bad Faeries.* Simon & Schuster.

Gager, J. G. (1992). *Curse Tablets and Binding Spells from the Ancient World*. Oxford University Press.

Gardner, G. (1954). *Witchcraft Today*. Rider and Company.

Giacomarra, M. G. (2012). *Hekate in the Greek and Roman World: Goddess of Witchcraft and Ghosts*. Archaeopress.

Goethe, J. W. (2014). *Faust, Part One* (D. Constantine, Trans.). Penguin Classics. (Original work published 1808)

Gow, A. S. F. (1950). *Theocritus* (Vol. 2). Cambridge University Press.

Graf, F. (1997). *Magic in the Ancient World* (F. Philip, Trans.). Harvard University Press.

Graves, R. (1955). *The Greek Myths*. Penguin Books.

Grayle, J. (2021). *Hekataeon*. Grayle Press.

Griffin, J. (1986). Greek Myth and Hesiod. In J. Boardman, J. Griffin, & O. Murray (Eds.), *The Oxford history of the Classical world* (pp. 78-98). Oxford University Press.

Grof, S. (1975). *Realms of the Human Unconscious: Observations from LSD Research*. Viking Press.

Guldager Bilde, P. (2009). Quantifying Black Sea Goddess: Some Thoughts on the Iconography of the Goddess with a Torch in the Chersonesean Sphere. In J. M. Højte (Ed.), *Mithridates VI and the Pontic Kingdom* (pp. 237-255). Aarhus University Press.

Harrison, J. E. (1903). *Prolegomena to the Study of Greek Religion.* Cambridge University Press.
Harrison, T. (1985). *Medea: A Sex-War Opera.* Bloodaxe Books.
Hatfield, G. (2004). *Encyclopedia of Folk Medicine: Old World and New World Traditions.* ABC-CLIO.
Hesiod. (2006). *Theogony, Works and Days, Testimonia* (G. W. Most, Ed. & Trans.). Harvard University Press. (Original work published ca. 700 BCE)
Hanegraaff, W. (2012) *Esotericism and the Academy,* Cambridge University Press
Heubeck, A., & Hoekstra, A. (1989). *A Commentary on Homer's Odyssey, Volume II: Books IX-XVI.* Oxford University Press.
Homer. (2003). *Homeric Hymns. Homeric Apocrypha. Lives of Homer* (M. L. West, Trans.). Loeb Classical Library.
Homer. (2018). *Odyssey* (E. Wilson, Trans.). W. W. Norton & Company. (Original work published ca. 8th century BCE)
Hunter, R. (2015). *Apollonius of Rhodes: Argonautica Book IV.* Cambridge University Press.
Johnston, S. I. (1990). *Hekate Soteira: A study of Hekate's Roles in the Chaldean Oracles and Related Literature.* Scholars Press.
Johnston, S. I. (1991). Crossroads. *Zeitschrift für Papyrologie und Epigraphik,* 88, 217-224.

Johnston, S. I. (1999). *Restless dead: Encounters Between the Living and the Dead in Ancient Greece*. University of California Press.
Johnston, S. I. (2008). *Ancient Greek Divination*. Wiley-Blackwell.
Jones, W. H. S. (Trans.). (1918). *Pausanias: Description of Greece*. Harvard University Press.
Jonson, B. (1972). The Masque of Queens. In S. Orgel (Ed.), *Ben Jonson: Complete Masques* (pp. 122-141). Yale University Press. (Original work published 1609)
Jordan, D. R. (1985). A Survey of Greek Defixiones Not Included in the Special Corpora. *Greek, Roman and Byzantine Studies*, 26, 151-197.
Karivieri, A. (2010). Magic and Syncretistic Religious Culture in the East. In J. Rüpke (Ed.), *A companion to Roman religion* (pp. 301-315). Wiley-Blackwell.
Kerényi, K. (1951). *The Gods of the Greeks*. Thames and Hudson.
Kingsley, P. (1995). *Ancient Philosophy, Mystery, and Magic: Empedocles and Pythagorean tradition*. Oxford University Press.
Kraus, T. (1960). *Hekate: Studien zu Wesen und Bild der Göttin in Kleinasien und Griechenland*. Carl Winter Universitätsverlag.
Laumonier, A. (1958). *Les Cultes Indigènes en Carie*. de Boccard.
Lee, K. H. (Ed.). (1997). *Euripides: Ion*. Aris & Phillips.

Lloyd-Jones, H. (Ed.). (1994). *Sophocles* (Vol. 20). Harvard University Press.

Lucian. (1925). *Dialogues of the Dead* (A. M. Harmon, Trans.). Loeb Classical Library.

Luck, G. (2006). *Arcana Mundi: Magic and the Occult in the Greek and Roman Worlds* (2nd ed.). Johns Hopkins University Press.

MacLachlan, B. (2007). Kore as Nymph, not Daughter: Persephone in a Locrian Cave. In M. Parca & A. Tzanetou (Eds.), *Finding Persephone: Women's rituals in the ancient Mediterranean* (pp. 215-236). Indiana University Press.

McPhee, B. D. (2020). *Blessed Heroes: Apollonius' Argonautica and the Homeric Hymns* [Doctoral dissertation, University of North Carolina at Chapel Hill].

Maehler, H. (Ed. & Trans.). (2004). *Bacchylides: A Selection*. Cambridge University Press.

Majercik, R. (1989). *The Chaldean Oracles: Text, translation, and commentary*. Brill.

Marquardt, P. A. (1981). A Portrait of Hecate. *American Journal of Philology*, 102(3), 243-260.

Maslow, A. H. (1964). *Religions, Values, and Peak Experiences*. Ohio State University Press.

Megaloudi, F. (2005). Burnt Sacrificial Plant Offerings in Hellenistic Times: An Archaeobotanical Case Study from Messene, Peloponnese, Greece. *Vegetation History and Archaeobotany*, 14, 329-340.

Merlin, M. D. (2003). Archaeological Evidence for the Tradition of Psychoactive Plant Use in the Old World. *Economic Botany*, 57(3), 295-323.

Middleton, T. (1993). The Witch. In P. Corbin & D. Sedge (Eds.), *Three Jacobean witchcraft plays* (pp. 85-142). Manchester University Press. (Original work published ca. 1616)

Mikalson, J. D. (2005). *Ancient Greek Religion*. Blackwell Publishing.

Mikalson, J. D. (2010). *Ancient Greek Religion* (2nd ed.). Wiley-Blackwell.

Mili, M. (2015). *Religion and Society in Ancient Thessaly*. Oxford University Press.

Miller, J. (2006). *Protection & Reversal Magick: A Witch's Defense Manual*. New Page Books.

Miller, J. (2010). *The Sorcerer's Secrets: Strategies in Practical Magick*. New Page Books.

Mitropoulou, E. (1978). *Triple Hekate Mainly in Votive Reliefs*. Pyli Publications.

Mylonas, G. E. (1961). *Eleusis and the Eleusinian Mysteries*. Princeton University Press.

Nilsson, M. P. (1967). *Geschichte der Griechischen Religion* (2nd ed., Vol. 1). C.H. Beck. (Original work published 1941)

Nock, A. D. (1972). *Essays on Religion and the Ancient World* (Z. Stewart, Ed.). Harvard University Press.

Ogden, D. (2002). *Magic, Witchcraft, and Ghosts in the Greek and Roman Worlds: A Sourcebook*. Oxford University Press.

Orr, E. R. (2007). *Druidry*. Piatkus Books.

Pakkanen, P. (1996). *Interpreting Early Hellenistic Religion: A Study Based on the Mystery Cult of Demeter and the Cult of Isis*. Finnish Academy of Science.

Parisinou, E. (2000). *The Light of the Gods: The Role of Light in Archaic and Classical Greek Cult*. Duckworth.

Parker, R. (2005). *Polytheism and Society at Athens*. Oxford University Press.

Pausanias. (1918). *Description of Greece* (W. H. S. Jones, Trans.). Harvard University Press. (Original work published 2nd century CE)

Petsalis-Diomidis, A. (2010). *Truly Beyond Wonders: Aelius Aristides and the Cult of Asklepios*. Oxford University Press.

Porphyry. (1983). *On Abstinence from Killing Animals* (G. Clark, Trans.). Duckworth. (Original work published 3rd century CE)

Porphyry. (2000). *On Images* (E. H. Gifford, Trans.). University of Michigan Press. (Original work published 3rd century CE)

Preisendanz, K. (1973). *Papyri Graecae Magicae: Die griechischen Zauberpapyri* (2nd ed.). Teubner.

Proclus. (2007). *Commentary on Plato's Timaeus* (H. Tarrant, Trans.). Cambridge University Press.

Rabinowitz, J. (1998). The Book of the Honey Bee Girl: Epithets of Hekate. *Classical Philology*, 93(1), 25-40.

Rabinowitz, J. (1998). *The Rotting Goddess: The Origin of the Witch in Classical Antiquity.* Autonomedia.

Rankine, D., & D'Este, S. (2009). *Practical Qabalah magick.* Avalonia.

Raubitschek, A. E. (1949). *Dedications from the Athenian Akropolis.* American School of Classical Studies at Athens.

Rayor, D. J. (Trans.). (2014). *The Homeric Hymns: A Translation, with Introduction and Notes.* University of California Press.

Regardie, I. (1971). *The Golden Dawn: An Account of the Teachings, Rites and Ceremonies of the Order of the Golden Dawn* (6th ed.). Llewellyn Publications. (Original work published 1937-1940)

Regardie, I. (1989). *The Golden Dawn: A complete course in practical ceremonial magic.* Llewellyn Publications.

Robert, L. (1955). *Hellenica: Recueil d'épigraphie, de Numismatique et d'Antiquités Grecques* (Vol. 10). Adrien-Maisonneuve.

Rohde, E. (1925). *Psyche: The Cult of Souls and Belief in Immortality Among the Greeks* (W. B. Hillis, Trans.). Routledge & Kegan Paul.

Roller, L. E. (1999). *In Search of God the Mother: The Cult of Anatolian Cybele.* University of California Press.

Ronan, S. (1992). The Goddess Hekate. In *The Goddess Hekate: Studies in Ancient Pagan and Christian Religion & Philosophy* (pp. 1-28). Chthonios Books.

Rose, H. J. (1950). *Handbook of Greek Mythology* (5th ed.). Methuen. (Original work published 1928)

Ruhl, S. (2009). *The Darkest Corner of the Woods*. Theatre Communications Group.

Sarian, H. (1992). Hekate. In *Lexicon Iconographicum Mythologiae Classicae* (Vol. 6, pp. 985-1018). Artemis Verlag.

Scarborough, J. (1991). The Pharmacology of Sacred Plants, Herbs, and Roots. In C. A. Faraone & D. Obbink (Eds.), *Magika hiera: Ancient Greek magic and religion* (pp. 138-174). Oxford University Press.

Schibli, H. S. (1993). Xenocrates' Daemons and the Irrational Soul. *Classical Quarterly*, 43(1), 143-167.

Schütz, K., Carle, R., & Schieber, A. (2006). Taraxacum — A Review on its Phytochemical and Pharmacological Profile. *Journal of Ethnopharmacology*, 107(3), 313-323.

Seneca. (2011). *Medea* (A. J. Boyle, Trans.). Oxford University Press. (Original work published 1st century CE)

Shakespeare, W. (2015). *Macbeth* (S. Clark & P. Mason, Eds.). Bloomsbury Arden Shakespeare. (Original work published ca. 1606)

Smith, K. M. (2016). *Hekate: A Symbol of the Dangers of Feminine Knowledge in Euripides* [Master's thesis, University of Kansas].

Smith, R. R. R. (1991). *Hellenistic Sculpture: A handbook*. Thames and Hudson.

Solmsen, F. (1979). *Isis Among the Greeks and Romans*. Harvard University Press.

Sommerstein, A. H. (Ed. & Trans.). (2001). *Aristophanes: Wealth*. Aris & Phillips.

Sommerstein, A. H. (Ed. & Trans.). (2008). *Aeschylus: Fragments*. Harvard University Press.

Starhawk, M. (1979). *The Spiral Dance: A Rebirth of the Ancient Religion of the Great Goddess*. Harper & Row.

Stepp, J. R. (2004). The Role of Weeds as Sources of Pharmaceuticals. *Journal of Ethnopharmacology*, 92(2-3), 163-166.

Stratton, K. B. (2007). *Naming the Witch: Magic, Ideology, and Stereotype in the Ancient World*. Columbia University Press.

Tarrant, H. (Trans.). (2007). *Proclus: Commentary on Plato's Timaeus, Volume 1*. Cambridge University Press.

Ustinova, Y. (2018). *Divine Mania: Alteration of consciousness in ancient Greece*. Routledge.

Valiente, D. (1962). *Where Witchcraft Lives*. Aquarian Press.

Valiente, D. (1975). *Natural Magic*. Robert Hale.

Valiente, D. (1983). *Witchcraft for Tomorrow*. Robert Hale.

Valamoti, S. M., Moniaki, A., & Karathanou, A. (2009). An Investigation of Processing and Consumption of Pulses Among Prehistoric Societies: Archaeobotanical, Experimental and Ethnographic Evidence from Greece. *Vegetation History and Archaeobotany*, 18, 55-73.

van Bremen, R. (2010). The Demes and Phylai of Stratonikeia in Karia. *Chiron*, 40, 271-290.
Vermeule, E. (1979). *Aspects of Death in Early Greek Art and Poetry*. University of California Press.
Von Rudloff, R. (1999). *Hekate in Ancient Greek Religion*. Horned Owl Publishing.
Wilber, K. (1977). *The Spectrum of Consciousness*. Quest Books.
Williamson, C. G. (2021). *Urban Rituals in Sacred Landscapes in Hellenistic Asia Minor*. Brill.
Zografou, A. (2010). *Chemins d'Hécate: Portes, Routes, Carrefours et Autres Figures de l'Entre-Deux*. Presses Universitaires de Liège.

When the sun sinks into the sea, and darkness broods over the land.. a subtle yet palpable transformation takes place. Good loses the battle over evil... and all manner of malevolent creatures rise from darkness... Worst of all are the human quislings, consorts of the devil, the witches, warlocks and sorcerers, who under the cover of the night tend their magical gardens, gather their herbs and create the poisons, potions and protections.

Lenni George is at least one of these... an active herbalist and potion maker; she grows her own magical plants and has created her own moon garden, dedicated to Hekate and a respect for older magical traditions. Lenni is intrigued by the paradoxes of Hekate as both a Chthonic and Ouranic goddess.

Lenni has been a lone practitioner for more than three decades. She is published on a wide range of topics from the PGM, to Hekate and dark botanical research and recipes.

She lives in Northern Italy with her husband and fellow magician Nat Clegg and their three cats. As a pedagogist, along with Nat, Lenni designs workshops and events on the Arts of Magic that are delivered in the UK, Italy and Greece.